Men-at-Arms • 6

The Austro-Hungarian Army of the Seven Years War

Albert Seaton • Illustrated by R Ottenfeld

Series editor Martin Windrow

First published in Great Britain in 1973 by Osprey Publishing,
PO Box 883, Oxford, OX1 9PL, UK
PO Box 3985, New York, NY 10185-3985, USA
Email: info@ospreypublishing.com

Osprey Publishing is part of the Osprey Group.

Transferred to digital print on demand 2014.

First published 1973
4th impression 2010

Printed and bound by PrintOnDemand-Worldwide.com, Peterborough, UK.

A CIP catalogue record for this book is available from the British Library.

ISBN: 978 0 85045 149 8

Series Editor: Martin Windrow

Note
In the preparation of this text acknowledgement is given to *Die Österreichische Armee*
by O. Teuber (Vienna 1895–1904) and the *History of Hungary* by D. Sinor (Allen &
Unwin 1959). All the photographs are reproduced courtesy of the Keeper, the Library
of the Victoria and Albert Museum (Photographer Berkhampsted Photographic,
Berkhampsted, Hertfordshire)

The Woodland Trust
Osprey Publishing is supporting the Woodland Trust, the UK's leading woodland
conservation charity, by funding the dedication of trees.

www.ospreypublishing.com

The Austro-Hungarian Army of the Seven Years War

Introduction

Austro-Hungary of the eighteenth century embraced numerous and diverse races, but the main political and ethnological components of the state were formed from the Duchy of Austria and the old Kingdoms of Bohemia and Hungary. Austria formed in addition the anchor sheet of the German Empire, its roots stretching back to Charlemagne's Holy Roman Empire. The Austrians, Czechs and Hungarians were of course separate peoples with no common origin or language.

Austria and the Holy Roman Empire

About two thousand years ago, the German peoples, leaving their Scandinavian homeland, crossed the Baltic and the North Sea and settled on the coast of the mainland, from where they made their way southwards up the Rhine to the source of the Danube. From there two Germanic tribes, the Cimbri and Teutoni, overran Celtic Gaul and invaded the Roman Empire in 109 B.C., being followed by successive waves of other Teuton barbarians, among whom were Suebi, Goths, Franks, Saxons, Alemans, Vandals, Lombards and Burgundians. In Caesar's time the Germanic Vindelici had already conquered and settled a large area south of the Danube, with their capital at Augsburg, stretching from Helvetia to what is now the Bavarian-Austrian frontier.

In the fourth century A.D. the Roman Emperor Constantine removed his capital from Rome to Byzantium and this eventually gave rise to the existence of two Roman Empires, that in the east centred on Constantinople, and that in the west with its capital remaining in Rome. Whereas the Western Empire was shortlived, breaking up

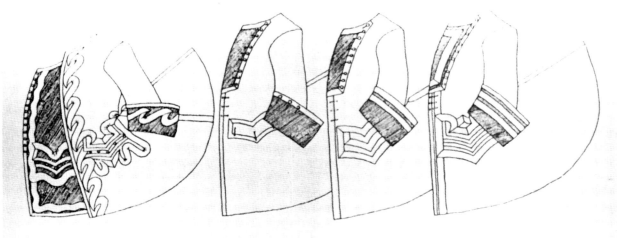

Feldmarschall   General de Bataille   Feldmarschall Lieutenant   Feldzeugmeister

Before Maria Theresa's reign there was neither a distinctive uniform nor badges of rank for general officers. These illustrate the first to be introduced, rank being shown by gold ribbon in the waistcoat and coat; ranks shown are field-marshal, major-general, general and master-general of ordnance

under the Hunnish and Vandal invasions, the Byzantine Empire was to endure for another thousand years.

The Christian Bishops of Rome, with the assistance of the Franks on whom they relied for protection against the Germanic Lombards, had meanwhile become the political rulers of Central Italy. In 768 Charlemagne, a German like his predecessors, came to the Frankish throne and for the next forty-three years dominated Europe, extending his own influence and that of the Roman Church. The Frankish kingdom already covered the whole of Gaul and the Low Countries, the north German coast as far as Denmark, and Central Germany, including what is now Bavaria and Upper Austria. In ceaseless and bloody wars against the North German Saxons, the Elbe Slavs and the Avar Kingdom on the middle Danube, Charlemagne pushed his frontiers eastwards as far as the Oder, the Bakony Forest (now Hungary) and the tongue of land between the Danube and the Sava on which Belgrade now stands. He annexed Slovenia, North and Central Italy, Corsica and a strip of borderland Spain as far south as Barcelona.

Before the end of the eighth century, Charlemagne regarded his domains as a revived Roman Empire and he opened negotiations with Constantinople in order to obtain recognition for himself as the Holy Roman Emperor in the West. In the autumn of 800 Charlemagne went to Italy to reinstate in his office Pope Leo III, who had been driven from Rome on a charge of evil living. There on Christmas Day Charlemagne was crowned Holy Roman Emperor by his vassal, Leo.

When Charlemagne died his Empire was divided among his sons and eventually became the Frankish and German kingdoms. Thereafter the Holy Roman Empire disintegrated as a political entity under the invasions of the Norsemen and the Hungarians. With the death in 919 of the last King of Germany directly descended from Charlemagne, the Saxons and the Franconians elected Henry the Fowler, Duke of Saxony, as King of the Germans. Henry's son, Otto the Great, crossed the Alps in 961 to restore order to the Roman Catholic Church, where the popes were once more in disrepute. He had himself crowned and demanded that henceforth no pope should be consecrated until he had first taken an oath of allegiance to the emperor. Otto the Great's Holy Roman Empire differed from that of Charlemagne since it included only Germany and North and Central Italy and had no claim on France or the borderlands of Spain.

Germany was developing very differently, however, from France and England in that it lacked the political unity usually associated with a kingdom, for it was in fact no more than a collection of independent or semi-independent principalities and duchies, and the kingship itself was strictly elective. A son might follow his father as king if he had reason to maintain his claim, but then only provided that the German princes were assured that he would be no threat to their independence. In consequence the kings were guided by their interests and those of their own duchies rather than by wider national issues. Often the title was one without substance. The Kings of Germany were the usual claimants of the Roman imperial title.

In the twelfth century Austria had been a tiny German duchy on the Danube to the east of Bavaria, hardly more than a hundred miles across, developed from Avar territory overrun and resettled by Charlemagne as part of the eastern frontier marches or Ostmark. The ruling dukes had originally come from Switzerland, taking their name of Habsburg, so it is said, from their family estates of Habichtsburg (Hawk's Castle) near Lake Lucerne. They extended their influence and domains throughout the eastern border provinces of Carinthia, Carniola, the Tyrol and Austria, usually by advantageous marriages. In 1273 Rudolf of Habsburg, Duke of Austria, was unanimously elected to the titles of the Holy Roman Empire, mainly on account of his lack of authority, means and pretensions; for, in spite of the elective principle, the earlier Hohenstaufen Emperors had in their time become very powerful. Under the first of the Habsburgs Germany and North Italy slipped back into anarchy and civil war, prince against prince and town against town.

Because of its internal weakness, Germany, and with it the Holy Roman Empire, began to move slowly eastwards. For a powerful France took advantage of the German confusion and began to annex the German territories of Flanders and

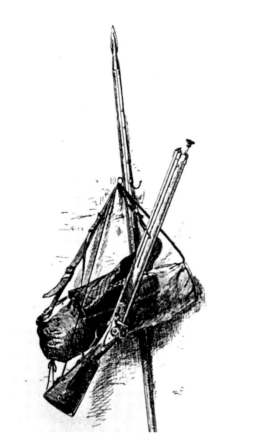

Equipment and arms of the border sharpshooter. The carbine is a twin (upper and lower) barrelled fire-arm, one barrel being rifled and the other smooth. The pike is fitted with an aiming rest for the carbine

Austrian institution, steadily rose while its power diminished, so that eventually it became merely of a traditional prestige importance. Even the papacy ceased to take an interest in it.

Yet the real power of the Austrian Habsburgs rested on foundations outside the German Holy Roman Empire. For the Habsburg Emperor Maximilian had married Mary of Burgundy, joining both Burgundy and the Belgian and Dutch Netherlands to his Austrian archduchy. Maximilian's and Mary's son, Philip the Fair of Burgundy, married Joanna of Castile, heiress to the whole of Spain, the Spanish New World in America and the southern half of Italy. And so Philip's eldest son, the Habsburg Holy Roman Emperor Charles V, inherited at the beginning of the sixteenth century a further empire, including Spain, Sardinia, Naples and Sicily, Milan, the Netherlands and Burgundy.

the Rhône Valley; with the passing of generations the German inhabitants became Frenchmen. Meanwhile, as if in compensation, German crusading bishops and knightly orders were already conquering the heathen-occupied territories to the east, in Brandenburg, Mecklenburg, Prussia and Silesia, and were resettling new villages and towns with German colonists.

The Golden Bull of 1356 reaffirmed the system of election to the crown of the Holy Roman Empire, vesting the right of election originally to seven of the great German princes, who thereafter became known as electors. Although from 1440 onwards it had become customary to elect a Habsburg to the throne, the electors were always in a position to extort concessions in exchange for their vote and the Habsburgs had to grant substantial monetary favours to ensure their own election. The expenses of the imperial crown, which was essentially a German and not an

The Coming of the Hungarians

No one knows with certainty from where the Hungarians came, for their origin is outside the European community of nations. Their Hungarian language is Ugrian, akin to the dialects spoken by the Ostiak and Vogul peoples of Western Siberia, and it is likely that the Hungarians once formed part of these races or had such prolonged contact with them that their tongues developed similarly. Another indication that the Hungarian tribes once lived on the frontier territories of Asia between the Volga and the Urals, is that their language includes commonplace words concerning livestock and agriculture borrowed from the Chuvash, a Turkish people still living in the Volga Basin near Kazan. The Hungarians have certain affinities, too, with the Turkish steppe tribes of southern Asia and this probably accounts for the confusion in identifying their early contacts with Byzantium and

Western Europe. For they were often called Turk, Bashkir, Sabir and Onogur. The latter name remained in constant use, however, and it is by this that the Hungarians are known to the western world today. The Hungarians call themselves Magyar, originally the name, not of the people, but of one of the main Hungarian tribes.

A loose association of Hungarian tribes emerged as nomadic horsemen on the great steppe plains in the south of Russia. They were forced westwards by the Turkish Pechenegs and, long before the end of the ninth century, had arrived in South-East Europe on the lower Danube. Leaving their temporary home between the lower Danube and the Pruth, the original seven Hungarian tribes, in all probably about a quarter of a million people, under a newly-elected Hungarian chieftain, Arpad, moved into the lowland areas of what is now Hungary.

Although ethnically far removed from the Avars and the Huns who had preceded them, and the Tartar Mongols who were yet to follow, the Hungarians were much akin to those peoples in their manners, customs and way of living. Even in the middle of the twelfth century the Hungarians still spent most of the year in tents, moving across the plains with great herds of horses seeking new pastures. They were a race of horsemen, and their light cavalry bowmen ranged far and wide in search of adventure and plunder. They were regarded by German, Slav and Italian as ferocious Asiatics for they raided and devastated Italy, plundering and burning great cities, and mounted annual campaigns which took them through Bavaria, Saxony and Thuringia as far west as Burgundy, the Rhone and the Pyrenees. To the south they ventured to Rome and Naples; to the north to Bremen. At first, the Germans were no match for the Hungarian horse, and Henry the Fowler, Duke of Saxony and King of Germany, had to pay tribute for nine years before he felt strong enough to defy them. Eventually, in 955, Otto the Great met and destroyed the Hungarian host at Lechfeld near Augsburg.

Although Lechfeld put an end to the Hungarian incursions into Western Europe it did nothing to ease the enmity between Magyar and German. Henceforth the Hungarians had to

A dragoon, c. 1770

combat German pressure and encroachment to the east.

THE ETHNOLOGICAL AND POLITICAL COMPLEXITY OF HUNGARY AND BOHEMIA

The Hungarian kingdom was far from being a national community, for it had admitted or conquered aliens who were never to be assimilated. The overrunning of Croatia and part of Dalmatia gave Hungary an outlet to the Adriatic, but it brought foreign peoples into the kingdom. In the north-east, along the Carpathians, part of Galicia was seized, together with its Russian (now Ukrainian) and Polish inhabitants. Hungary owes its multi-racial character principally, however, to the Mongol-Tartar occupation of 1241–1242, for the devastated and depopulated areas of

Central Hungary and Transylvania were resettled by Turkish Comans, Rumanian, German, Polish and Russian immigration. In Transylvania and South Hungary, in particular, these new populations soon outnumbered the Hungarian hosts. Much later large Serbian populations were admitted.

In the north-west of Hungary lay the Czech Kingdom of Bohemia, with its capital at Prague, together with the state of Moravia, the remnant of an ancient and larger kingdom with a mainly Slovak population, and the Slav province of Silesia, inhabited principally by Sorbs and Poles together with strong German colonies. Silesia had originally belonged to Poland, but by the end of the fifteenth century it formed, together with Moravia, part of the Bohemian Kingdom, temporarily linked with Hungary under a common monarch.

With the death of the last of the Arpad dynasty in 1301, the Hungarian kingship had become elective. Over the last century or so there had been a change in the pattern of Hungarian society. The tribal organization and nomadic habits had been lost, and wealth and power were now based on the ownership of land. With the creation of the barons came a new nobility and attendant serfdom. The first of the elected kings, Charles Robert of Anjou, set up the French feudal military organization of the *banderia*, whereby each noble had to furnish an armed contingent recruited from his retainers and serfs. This was the forerunner of the *insurrectio*, Hungarian troops raised by the nobility for the defence of the realm.

The crowns of Poland and Bohemia were similarly elective and the barons there, known as the magnates, were equally determined to prevent any single family holding the throne by hereditary right. The rule of strong monarchs, particularly if they were kings of a Bohemian-Polish or Polish-Hungarian union, brought temporary stability and held in check the bitter rivalries of Hungary, Bohemia and Poland for the control of South-East Europe, a rivalry complicated by the effect of the multi-national colonization. Under weaker kings the powerful magnates brought their countries to a state of anarchy.

The common people had been largely reduced to serfdom. Their situation in Hungary was particularly bad since the baron's diet of 1492 had enacted that no peasant *jobbagy* could move his residence without the consent of his lord. In accordance with the *Tripartitum* of 1515, the diet further decreed that no noble could be arrested before judgement, that the king could do nothing detrimental to the noble's person or property without legal proceedings, that no noble should pay any taxes or tolls and only in the case of a defensive war had the noble any obligation of military service. The nobles were thus given rights without duties; the *jobbagy* on the other hand fought for the king and paid for the wars. The situation continued to exist unchanged throughout the eighteenth century.

Herberstein, the Holy Roman Emperor's ambassador to Hungary, described the nobility of the period in unflattering terms, 'disunited, vain and arrogant, each seeking his own profit and living on the fat of public property, corrupt, haughty and proud, unable to command or to obey; unwilling to accept advice, working little but spending their time with feasting and intriguing'.

A driver of the pontoon train, c. 1770

7

The Austro-Hungarian Union

In 1526 the Turkish Sultan Soliman II, having already taken Belgrade, advanced northwards up the Danube Valley and destroyed the Hungarian Royal Army at Mohacs. There the Hungarian King, Louis II, lost his life. The detail of the Turkish occupation and the dynastic struggles in West and Central Europe are complicated and of no concern here. It suffices that the claimant of the Hungarian throne, Ferdinand Habsburg, Archduke of Austria and brother of the Imperial Emperor Charles V, unable to drive back the Turk, contrived to occupy and rule over only a narrow strip of Hungarian border territory in the west and north. The Turkish Sultan, encouraged by French enmity to the Habsburgs, took possession of the remainder, first setting up a rival Hungarian king and then, finally, incorporating it into the Ottoman Empire. Transylvania, under a Hungarian ruler or *voivode*, became a Turkish vassal state.

When the Habsburg Emperor Charles V abdicated in 1556 he left his Spanish, Italian and Netherland possessions to his son, Philip II of Spain (husband of Mary Tudor). His Austrian and German territories went to his brother Ferdinand, who succeeded as Holy Roman Emperor. The Austrian Habsburgs continued to prosper in the sixteenth and seventeenth centuries, however, becoming Kings of Bohemia, together with Moravia and Silesia, and in 1699, when the Turks were finally driven off to the south, the *de facto* rulers of Hungary and Transylvania.

Ferdinand I, the first Habsburg King of Hungary, had a Spanish mother and a Spanish education, and he understood no Hungarian. The provincial town of Pressburg (Pozsony), originally selected as a capital since Buda was held by the Turks, was too small to house the Hungarian royal court and so Ferdinand dispensed with it, ruling his Austrian Archduchy and Hungarian Kingdom from Vienna through the Austrian Royal Council, the *Hofrat*. Since the Hungarians stiffly refused to be represented on this German institution they had little say in major policy and none in foreign affairs. As Kings of Hungary and Bohemia, successive Austrian Habsburgs were already head of a multi-lingual and multi-national state which had its roots in Eastern Europe and the Balkans; it was impossible to reconcile the conflicting views and interests of their subjects. Yet, as Emperors of Germany and zealous Roman Catholics, the greater part of Habsburg energies were directed northwards where German protestant princes, encouraged by France, Denmark and Sweden, were ready to wage war against Austria, Bavaria and the papacy in defence of their religion and local liberties. For one of the causes of the disastrous Thirty Years War in Germany (1618–1648) had been the rejection by the Habsburg Emperor Ferdinand II of the provisions of the 1555 Treaty of Augsburg, a compromise whereby the religion of any particular German state was to be determined by that of its ruler. For Ferdinand, intent on a Roman Catholic revival, stifled protestantism in Austria and Bohemia and wanted to enforce a similar policy on his neighbours.

A hussar in parade order, c. 1770

AUSTRO-HUNGARY IN THE EIGHTEENTH CENTURY

When Charles II, the last Habsburg monarch of Spain, died in 1700 without an heir, he left his dominions to Philip of Anjou, a grandson of the French monarch, Louis Bourbon. Fearing a union of France and Spain under a common Bourbon monarch, the Austrian Emperor formed the Grand Alliance with England and Holland to fight what became known as the War of the Spanish Succession. The Austrian troops, under Prince Eugène, and Austria's allies under Marlborough, won Blenheim in 1704 and invaded France and Spain. Mutual exhaustion ended the war in 1713, with the Peace of Utrecht. In Europe Austria was the victor and Spain the loser. For the Habsburgs held Hungary, Croatia and Transylvania, the Austrian lands of Upper and Lower Austria, Carinthia, Carniola, Tyrol, Breisgau, Burgau, Moravia, Silesia and Bohemia; in addition the Treaty of Utrecht gave them the Belgian Netherlands, Naples, Sardinia and Milan. More than a third of the German territory of the Holy Roman Empire was now ruled directly from Vienna. Austria ranked with France and Britain as one of the most powerful states in Europe.

Meanwhile, however, the relationship between Austria and Hungary had deteriorated once more, the Hungarian rebels under Rakoczi refusing to recognize the Habsburg hereditary claim to the throne of Hungary or the separation of Transylvania from Hungary (it was now ruled direct from Vienna). The Treaty of Szatmar, which put an end to the rebellion but did little to alleviate grievances, coincided with the accession in 1711 of the Emperor Charles VI (Charles III of Hungary).

In contrast to his predecessors, Charles showed much goodwill towards his non-Germanic subjects and in particular towards the Hungarians. Since Charles was the last surviving male member of the Habsburg line he required the acceptance by the Hungarians and Bohemians of the 1713 Pragmatic Sanction which extended the provisions of a former family agreement so that Charles's daughters should become heirs to the throne. This was eventually accepted and a defensive union was established between Austria,

Green-coated light horse, the successors to the horse-grenadiers, c. 1770

Bohemia and Hungary through the person of the Emperor. One of the most important measures passed by the Hungarian Diet between 1715 and 1722 was the establishing of a common Austro-Hungarian standing army, since the Hungarian *insurrectio* could hardly be called a trained and disciplined force. Since the *insurrectio*, the almost fictional noble levy, theoretically remained in being as the national Hungarian army, conscripts for the Austro-Hungarian Army were, more often than not, incorporated into the Germanic military organization of the Empire, mostly under German officers using German words of command. Once again the Hungarian nobility was exempted from taxation and military service and the burden of filling the conscription and paying for the new army rested on the *jobbagy*.

The policy-making body for the government of Hungary remained the Viennese Hofkammer ruling through the Hungarian Chancellery, also in the Austrian capital, which was in effect the intermediary between king and nation. Its executive in Buda, known as the *helytartotanacs*, was nominated by the king and had no connection with the diet, which was responsible only for the voting of war taxes. The administration of the taxes and all other financial questions were in the hands of the *kamara* which was answerable only to the Viennese Hofkammer.

Two more wars were fought against the Turks in 1716 and 1736. In the first, Temesvar in the south-east of Hungary was finally freed from occupation and Belgrade and the northern Balkans were taken by Austro-Hungarian troops under the leadership of the veteran Prince Eugène of Savoy. As a result of the second war, however, many of these former gains were lost.

Brandenburg-Prussia Challenges Austria

As Holy Roman Emperor, Charles VI had his own separate machinery of German imperial government with a diet in Ratisbon representing the members of the three colleges (*curiae*) of electors, princes and imperial cities, but these were merely debating delegates from independent states. For in spite of the fact that the 1648 settlement recognized only the territorial supremacy (*Landeshoheit*) of the rulers, they still enjoyed undisputed and complete sovereignty. The diet concerned itself with little of importance and its decisions had only marginal effect since there was no means of forcing their implementation. There was no standing imperial defence force, since the existence of such an army depended on contributions. The empire was divided into ten regions or circles but across these administrative borders ran a patchwork of more than 300 sovereign German states, large and small. The most important of these, in addition to Austria, were Bavaria, Saxony and Prussia.

Prussia had developed from the Electorate of Brandenburg, increasing in area during the seventeenth century by the acquisition of Cleves, Mark and Ravensburg, East Pomerania, Halberstadt, Minden and Magdeburg. Many of these states were scattered throughout Germany and it became the ambition of the Brandenburg Electors to unite them. The Elector also owned Prussia (later known as East Prussia), lying to the east of the Vistula outside the border of the German Empire, the area of which was almost two thirds as great as that of Brandenburg. From 1701 onwards the Elector of Brandenburg was also styled the King of Prussia.

To King Frederick William I, the father of Frederick the Great, Prussia owed its centralized military form of government, a large and well trained army (Prussian contingents fought at Blenheim, Ramillies and Oudenarde), popular schools, an efficient civil service and a well ordered fiscal system. Under such a administration the Prussian population grew up inured to hardship and glorifying in austerity, obedience and duty. In spite of extensive immigration schemes to attract West German and Dutch settlers to open up the barren and sandy wasteland and reclaim the marshes (about twenty per cent of the Prussian-Brandenburgers were such immigrants), the total population of Prussia and all its dependencies hardly numbered much more than four and a half million. The population of the

Hussar officer in undress uniform

territories of the Austrian Habsburgs was about twenty-five million, ten million within and fifteen million without the borders of the Empire.

Frederick William believed that Prussia must expand or stagnate and in 1728 he made an agreement with the Emperor Charles VI by which he was to be guaranteed the West German Duchy of Berg on the death of its ruler, in return for Prussia's adherence to the Pragmatic Sanction assuring the female succession to the Austrian possessions. Spain and Russia were already signatories and Britain and France became additional guarantors a few years later. After securing signatures from the major European powers, Charles VI had misgivings about his earlier undertaking to support the transfer of Berg to Prussia. Frederick William, nursing a grievance, came to a secret understanding with France.

When Frederick the Great came to the throne shortly afterwards he inherited both the agreement with France and the Prussian hostility to Austria.

German infantry, a drummer, fusilier and a grenadier

A few months later, in October 1740, the Emperor Charles VI died and his daughter Maria Theresa, a young married woman of twenty-three years of age, succeeded him.

Frederick immediately invaded Austrian Silesia, and the war began between Prussia and Austria which was to become the struggle for the mastery of Germany. Unexpectedly, it was Hungary that came to Austria's aid.

The War of the Austrian Succession

Frederick the Great was arbiter of his own fate, from the time of his accession accountable to none. In going to war he was certainly not entirely motivated by spite against Austria; he may or may not have wanted to cut a dashing figure on the contemporary political scene, but primarily he was an opportunist guided by what he judged to be Prussian interests, and the European field was clear for ambition. He was untroubled and uninhibited by conscience, by a standard of common decency or by any fellow feeling for his brother Germans outside of Prussia. He was perfidious, irreligious and cynical; for him the end justified the means. He rightly judged Austro-Hungary, in spite of its size and large population, to be disunited and militarily weak, and he was correct in believing that the political climate in Europe was auspicious for an unprovoked attack. He was wrong, however, in his assessment of the energy, strength and wisdom of the new Austrian ruler, by far the most distinguished monarch the Habsburgs ever produced, and in the fervent support she was to receive, as Queen of Hungary, from the Hungarian people.

Frederick attacked Silesia because he wanted its rich territory. The province was contiguous to Brandenburg, and brought to him further political and strategic advantages in that it cut off the Elector of Saxony, who was also King of Poland, from his territories in the east. Silesia outflanked

Western Poland, also coveted by Frederick. Anxious for a share in the spoils, France demanded the Austrian Netherlands and Luxembourg while the Elector of Bavaria claimed the imperial crown. Franco-Bavarian troops invaded Austria and Bohemia, threatening Vienna and taking Prague. England and Holland, as usual, sided against the French and sent an annual subsidy to Vienna.

The War of the Austrian Succession, in so far as it concerns operations in Central Europe, embraces what is usually referred to as the First and the Second Silesian Wars.

The First Silesian War

Before Frederick the Great entered Silesia he had made his preparations in the greatest of secrecy, cloaking all activity in the guise of a march to be made to the west to secure the provinces of Jülich-Berg on the Rhine, already promised to his father. In December 1740 the main body of the 28,000 strong Prussian force crossed into Silesia; Frederick himself assumed full control and Count von Schwerin, who had been commander-in-chief up to this time, was relegated to the command of a division. The hereditary Prince of Anhalt-Dessau (the Young Dessauer) was to follow from Berlin with a further 12,000 men.

A month before, the Austrian force in Silesia, which had numbered barely 600 horse and 3,000 foot, was under the command of the military governor, Count von Wallis, a soldier of Scottish descent whose forbears had come to Austria generations before. Wallis had been surprised by the outbreak of the new war and, having received neither aid nor instructions from Vienna, prepared for siege the nearby town of Glogau, said to be the key to North Silesia, with the only troops he had readily to hand, about 1,000 men. Wallis was a man of energy and he had brought in from the surrounding countryside salt, meat and meal,

constructed trenches and palisades and burned down the suburbs to create fields of fire. And yet war was still conducted according to the peculiar mid-eighteenth century rules of Austrian formalism, for when Wallis proposed to blow up the Protestant church outside the town, 'in case the Prussians make a blockhouse out of it', the chief Protestant burgher in Glogau pleaded against this action and was sent to Frederick by Wallis for a written undertaking that the church would not be used by the military. This the King readily gave and the church was spared.

Meanwhile Wallis's deputy, a General Count von Browne, a German-Irish Roman Catholic descendant of an exiled Jacobite, born in Basle in 1705 and cousin of Field-Marshal Browne, Governor of Riga in the Russian service, happened to be in the south; he began to draw in detached units from Moravia and South Silesia until eventually he had concentrated 7,000 foot. But

A collection of hussar arms and accoutrements

many of these he dissipated, in accordance with the military code at the time, by allocating them to fortresses and strongholds, keeping only 600 dragoons under his own hand. The sectional interests of the Silesian people proved recalcitrant and obstructive, and Browne was obliged to abandon Breslau, the capital, to its own devices. Wallis sent a messenger to Frederick warning him that if he attacked Glogau 'it would be most resolutely defended'; so the King, having inspected the defences from afar, marched on, leaving the Young Dessauer to mask the town with part of the reserve 'but not attack'. The Prussian force marched on in two columns, Frederick with the larger and Schwerin with the smaller, the town of Liegnitz being taken by Schwerin by a *coup de main*. Browne and his elusive flying cavalry column had not been idle, for he visited and encouraged his numerous garrisons and detachments. The first of these, only 260 stout-hearted Austrian grenadiers at Ottmachau on the Neisse, held out against Frederick for three days before being reduced by bombardment. Von Roth, the Austrian commander at Neisse, held out successfully so that Frederick had to be content with another masking blockade as at Glogau and Brieg. The rest of Silesia had for the time being been overrun by Prussian troops so that Browne was forced to withdraw into Moravia.

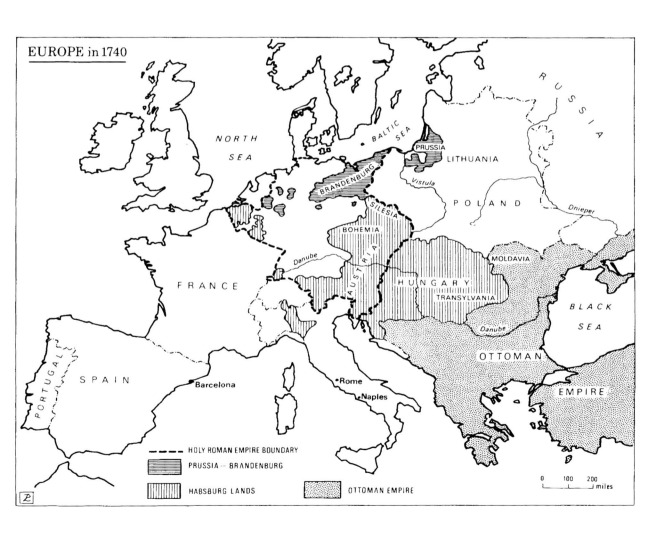

EUROPE in 1740

HOLY ROMAN EMPIRE BOUNDARY
PRUSSIA — BRANDENBURG
HABSBURG LANDS
OTTOMAN EMPIRE

0   100   200 miles

Frederick, who had returned to Berlin expecting to hear from diplomatic channels that the war was won, learned, to his chagrin, that the Austrians were mobilizing in earnest. He set out almost immediately for Silesia. There Browne and Lentulus had established themselves in Glatz and were infiltrating regular and irregular troops back into Silesia. About 600 men had forced their way through the blockading Prussians and reinforced the Austrian garrison at Neisse. The Silesian roads and backwoods had become infested with irregulars, both foot and horse, principally Hungarian and Serbo-Croat pandours (a corruption from *banderia*) and Magyar hussars. These latter were not necessarily part of the regular forces since they were, more often than not, irregular light horse or part of the *insurrectio* enlisted for the purpose.

In Prussian eyes the pandour-hussars were indisciplined predators, but they gave endless trouble, cutting off detachments and murdering the wounded. Indeed, they were so bold that scores of them would hang about the Prussian encampments in broad daylight, just outside musket range, watching and reporting all movement and activity. They were no match against disciplined Prussian infantry, but so great was the self-esteem of the Magyar horsemen, that they were not afraid to attack Prussian cavalry. At one time they put to flight a squadron of Schulenburg Dragoons which served as the royal escort, and the King of Prussia himself was nearly taken. The pandours were excellent in collecting information and denying the enemy reconnaissance, so that, even in those areas where the population was Protestant and friendly, it became difficult for the Prussians to learn what was going on in Silesia. Beyond the borders it was impossible. When a new Austrian army under Neipperg entered Silesia on its way to relieve the town of Neisse, the Austrian field-marshal, in the words of one chronicler, 'walked invisible within clouds of pandours'.

Frederick, by rare good fortune, first heard of Neipperg's approach from Austrian deserters. Glogau had already been taken by the Young Dessauer in a night action, which lasted only an hour, hardly fifty men being lost by either side. The Brieg blockade was given up and Frederick prepared to meet the oncoming Austrians.

MOLLWITZ

Although it was already the first week in April, two feet of snow lay on the ground. Neipperg's headquarters had reached a small hamlet called Mollwitz and his army lay there and in the area of two adjacent towns of Langwitz and Grüningen, astride Frederick's communications to the Prussian reserves and magazines at Ohlau. Neipperg's mounted pandours had captured all the Prussian messengers sent by Frederick to bring up reinforcements. At daybreak on Monday 10 April Frederick, who was near Brieg, still did not know the whereabouts of the Austrians, although they were in fact only seven miles away, until one of his General-Adjutants chanced to ask a passing Silesian labourer if he had heard where the Austrians were. This farm servant knew full well (*recht gut*) and, on invitation, acted as the Prussian guide.

Neipperg, the Austrian commander, was just sitting down to dinner at the house of the Bürgermeister of Mollwitz when the firing of outpost

A German fusilier

signal rockets warned him that something was afoot. A hussar party was sent out; this came back at the gallop with von Rothenburg's Prussian dragoons hard on its heels. Neipperg called for Römer, his Saxon General of Horse, the alarm was sounded, and the troops sent for from the outlying villages. By then the Prussians were already deploying in two lines about 300 yards apart (just beyond musket range so that they should not be hit in each other's fire), each line consisting of three ranks.

Neipperg had about 20,000 troops, although many of these were slow arriving on the field. The Prussians had somewhat more. The Austrians deployed 8,600 regular cavalry of good quality, outnumbering the Prussian horse by two to one; the Austrian artillery, however, was weak, only eighteen pieces to the Prussian sixty. Neipperg's deployment was in the orthodox military fashion, in two lines, exactly the same as the Prussian, having a frontage of perhaps two miles in length. The left wing under Römer formed up first, its infantry element being commanded by Goldlein, a Swiss; the right wing, when assembled, was to be under Neipperg.

At two o'clock that afternoon all sixty Prussian guns opened a rapid and sustained fire on the Austrian left, with very damaging effect to horse standing in line. Neipperg was far away on the extreme Austrian right, still engaged in bringing troops in the field. Römer could get no orders. The counter-bombardment fire was weak and the Austrian horse became first restless and then angry. 'Are we to be shot down like dogs! For God's sake lead us forward!' Römer could hold them no longer and gave the order to advance. The thirty squadrons fell on the Prussian ten squadrons, five of them Schulenburg's Dragoons, and caught them in the flank as they were changing position. The Prussian cavalry, of indifferent quality, was unschooled in close-quarter fighting. Austrian and Hungarian discharged his pistol and then set to with sabre, the first slash to the horse's head and the second to the rider as the horse went down. Schulenburg was slashed twice and went down for ever. Within minutes the Prussian horse was ruined and in flight, hotly chased between its own lines of infantry while the pursuing Austrians rode the gauntlet of musketry fire. It left the field.

Römer took nine of the Prussian guns and turned his intrepid horse against the infantry line. Römer and many of his companions were killed in the infantry fire but the cavalry regrouped in excellent order preparatory to charging once more. At this stage it looked as if the Prussians were lost and Frederick their King fled the field of this, his first battle, to Oppeln thirty-five miles away. Many of his escort were cut down or captured by Hungarian hussar or pandour. The command of the remaining infantry force was left to Schwerin.

The Prussian infantry, most of it drilled for twenty years but never in action before, stood firm in that great surging sea of horse. Neipperg ordered Goldlein's foot forward to dislodge the Prussians. Goldlein fell at the first Prussian volley. The design of the Prussian muskets with their iron ramrods was much superior to that of the Austrian, with double the rate of fire, and the white-coated attackers were unable to get to bayonet distance. Only artillery grape could have blown the Prussian away. The Austrian horse, however, continued to charge the infantry lines, five times during the next four hours, until dispirited and raked by musketry, they, too, had to fall back. Schwerin's ammunition was running low and between cavalry charges foragers were running out collecting ball and powder from the slain. At seven o'clock, just before sunset, Schwerin sensed he had the advantage and ordered the advance. Neither Austrian horse nor foot would accept further battle, and they trooped off the field. There was never any question of pursuit, for the Austrian cavalry was too strong, but the Prussians remained encamped on the field of battle. They had lost in killed, wounded and missing 4,600 men, against an Austrian loss of 4,400.

Neipperg should have won Mollwitz and nearly did so, in spite of his inferior infantry and artillery. He failed because the Austrian way of conducting war was too confident, indolent and leisurely; all ranks shared a traditional and misplaced contempt for Prussia. On leaving for the battle, Neipperg's staff officers had told their hosts to keep the dishes hot 'for we will be back soon after we have brushed the Prussians' jackets for them'. Reconnaissance and intelligence had been neglected. On the Sunday, the day before the battle, there had been severe snowstorms which had

A three-pounder gun team in action, the *Kanonier***, who is the number one and the gun-layer, being astride the mounting.**

The *Besteck* **sling over his left shoulder is clearly visible**

reduced visibility to twenty yards and this may have accounted for the scouts and pandours not being at their posts. But to have allowed Frederick to have made his approach march unobserved was hardly to be forgiven. Had it not been that Frederick was new to warfare and that Schwerin was a soldier of the old school, the Prussians might have gone in to the attack without the lengthy deployment into line; then Neipperg's surprised troops would have been routed.

CHOTUSITZ

Frederick remained at Strehlen about twenty miles from Brieg bringing in reinforcements and reforming and retraining his cavalry. About six years before he had detached some officers, among them the Captain Ziethen afterwards to become so famous, to the Austrian cavalry to learn what was known as the hussar art. Hussars were originally Hungarian light cavalry, in some respects akin to the Turkish uhlan. The name appears to have come from the old Slavonic or Serbian *husar* or *gusar*, but its meaning and earlier origin are obscure. It might have meant 'a gooseherd' although there is some reason for believing that it was a Serbian corruption of the

old Italian *corsare*. The hussar, by degrees, had become the Austrian light horse factotum; for though he was in all respects a cavalryman of the line, he specialized in scouting, deep penetration, convoying and in combating partisans and enemy hussars.

After Mollwitz Frederick began the systematic retraining of his own horse in order to match it against the Austrian line cavalry and prepare it for operations against the Magyar hussars and pandours.

Neipperg remained in Neisse until August and for the next three months marched and counter-marched, trying to destroy the Prussian maga-zines. But meanwhile Maria Theresa, anxious to start operations against the Franco-Bavarians, had, much against her will, begun negotiations with Frederick. Frederick and Neipperg met in strict secrecy near Neisse and there the King of Prussia played false to his allies. By the Convention of Klein Schnellendorf, Frederick agreed to conduct sham skirmishes and sieges in order to deceive the French, but in reality to withdraw Prussia from the war. In return, he demanded that he be left in possession of his Silesian spoils. To this Maria Theresa agreed, possibly in no good faith, so that Austria might split its enemies and deal with the Bavarian, French and Saxon forces in Bohemia. Neipperg's troops then withdrew from Silesia.

However, the Franco-Bavarian troops appeared to have had little difficulty in overrunning Bohemia. Frederick, incensed by jealousy and surprised at what he believed to be the Austrian weakness, went back on his secret agreement and ordered the occupation of Glatz and Moravia. But once in Moravia, Frederick received little help from the French, who soon withdrew. The Slovak inhabitants were hostile and the pandours were everywhere, giving the Saxons in particular a rough handling. Frederick was unable to take Brünn and the Saxons departed for home, thus causing a permanent breach in Prusso-Saxon relations. The discomfited Frederick was forced to retire to Bohemia. There he was met at Chotusitz by a 30,000 strong Austrian Army under Maria Theresa's brother-in-law, Prince Charles of Lorraine.

The village of Chotusitz was held by the Young Dessauer, his infantry drawn up, as usual, in two lines. Frederick with the foot grenadiers, the horse and much of the artillery was to his right. Charles of Lorraine advanced, his infantry likewise in two lines, with cavalry on both flanks edging forward so that the battle formation was in a crescent pattern. Frederick followed the sequence of battle as at Mollwitz, his artillery playing on the Austrian cavalry flank, but with the difference that it was the Prussian horse which first rode into the attack. The Austrian first and

Detail of the 1760 three-pounder field gun. Until 1770 about four-fifths of Austrian artillery was made up of three-pounders

second line of cavalry broke. The Austrian infantry in the centre, little daunted, marched straight into Chotusitz where the broken ground and ditches made it impossible for Frederick's cavalry to penetrate. The fiercest of infantry fighting took place in the village, the Austrians losing heavily, 'rushing on like lions, shot down in ranks, whole swaths of dead men, and their muskets by them!' The Austrian left was already in a bad way; the right was in good condition, but the wings were now separated by the burning village. The indisciplined Habsburg horse was plundering the Prussian rear. A final Prussian attack with guns and infantry on the faltering left decided the day and at noon Charles gave the order to retreat. He had lost eighteen guns and nearly half his men, although many of these were stragglers or deserters.

The Austrian infantry had fought not with their customary obstinacy, but with fury. After the battle the belief took hold, not only abroad but in Vienna, that the Prussians were invincible. Maria Theresa decided to sue for peace, and by the Treaty of Berlin in July 1742 marked the end of the First Silesian War. This took Frederick speedily out of a European War which he had himself started, together with the only spoils. Saxony went out of the war with him. Austro-Hungarian troops then cleared Bohemia of the French and invaded Bavaria, driving the Elector, who had meanwhile been crowned as Holy Roman Emperor, from his own Munich capital. The Anglo-Hanoverians, together with the Austrians, won Dettingen, and France was forced back on the defensive. Maria Theresa prepared to conquer Alsace.

Frederick of Prussia had no wish to see France forced out of the war since this would, he believed, leave him alone to face Austria. He suspected that Maria Theresa's cession of Silesia was merely an arrangement of convenience until Bavaria, France and Spain were beaten. Frederick hastened to ally himself again by the Union of Frankfurt to Bavaria, to the Palatine and Hesse-Cassel, and to France, to uphold the authority of the imperial crown worn temporarily by Charles Albert of Bavaria. This was meant as a counter to Austria. As soon as the Austrian forces had entered Alsace, Frederick invaded Bohemia once more.

The Second Silesian War

In August 1744 Frederick set 80,000 Prussians on the march towards Prague and had a further 20,000 in reserve in Silesia. Prague itself was garrisoned by 4,000 Austrian troops and about 10,000 local levies. Maria Theresa went once more to Pressburg to appeal to the Hungarian nation for help and Charles of Lorraine was ordered to march out of Alsace eastwards.

By the first week in September Frederick's siege-artillery had arrived by Elbe barge and the cannonade of the city began. The Austrian batteries were overwhelmed and after a week the Austrian commander, General Harsch, surrendered. Two days later Frederick, Schwerin and the Young Dessauer were on the march again towards Tabor and Austria. It appeared that nothing could withstand them.

The tide of battle changed, however, with the reappearance of the clouds of Hungarian horse and pandours. The Prussians were soon in a difficult position. Unlike the Silesian, the local population was hostile, fleeing the path of the invader and removing or destroying provisions. The irregular Magyar horse and pandours insolently enclosed encampments and columns, controlled the highways and captured all messengers, so that for a whole month Frederick was out of touch from his kingdom and the rest of Europe, with no news of friend or foe.

During this time Charles of Lorraine had been marching hard from the west, having broken contact with the French, and he arrived in Bohemia in the early October, together with Field-Marshal von Traun, an experienced Austrian who was his deputy and principal adviser. They made their way to the Elbe, not far from Kolin, where they were joined by 20,000 Saxons. Frederick was already in danger of being cut off from Prague, and the 20,000 Prussians remaining in the Bohemian capital were threatened. In order to keep the way open to Prague, Frederick moved across the Moldau; the crossing of this river cost him seven hours of bitter fighting against the swarms of pandours.

Traun had skilfully evaded Frederick's efforts to bring him to a pitched battle on ground of Prussian choosing but then, in the early hours of 19 November, Austrians and Saxons crossed the Elbe by stealth and attacked the Prussians on the south bank. The woods were beset with infiltrating pandours 'uttering their blood-curdling shrieks'; every Prussian scout, every messenger sent out was killed. Amid fierce and scattered fighting the Prussians were worsted and Frederick determined on a retreat out of Bohemia. Numbers of guns were spiked and enormous quantities of small arms thrown into the river; powder and supplies were destroyed. The Prussian field army and garrisons made their way back to Silesia, harried both by irregulars and the populace, and continually fighting as their progress was barred by Austrian and Saxon regular forces. Losses in casualties, deserters and equipment were heavy. Afterwards Frederick was to say that he considered Traun's conduct of the campaign 'a model of perfection'.

Traun then invaded Silesia with 20,000 regular forces and a large body of irregulars, but he was mainly intent on giving as much trouble to the Old Dessauer who was in command, without being himself pinned and brought to battle. The effectiveness of the pandours may be gauged in that Frederick, when he wanted to send a letter to Jägerndorf ordering back a 12,000-strong Prussian detachment, had to entrust the message to Ziethen, with his great reputation as a skirm-

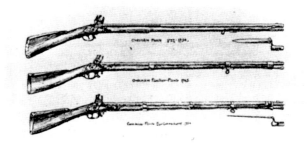

General Service flint-lock muskets with bayonets; the *ordinär* remained in service until 1754 when it was gradually replaced by the *Commiss-Flinte*. The *Füsilier-Flinte* was an interim substitute which was itself replaced by the 1754 pattern firearm

isher and backwoodsman, and no fewer than 500 Prussian hussars. Even this force, although travelling at speed by carefully chosen and little used routes was eventually brought to a halt and furiously set on by the irregulars, so that it had to be extricated by the Jägerndorf garrison. By now yet another mounted irregular had appeared, the Polish uhlan light horse, usually in Saxon pay.

Meanwhile Charles Albert of Bavaria had died, and the resilient and energetic Maria Theresa, who had already detached the Saxons to her cause, invaded Bavaria, inducing the new Elector to support her husband's nomination to the imperial crown.

HOHENFRIEDBERG AND SOHR

Maria Theresa intended to invade Silesia in May 1745, but she erred in entrusting the command to Charles of Lorraine rather than to Traun. By the clever use of an unsuspecting double spy Frederick had led Charles to believe that if Silesia were to be attacked by the Austrians, the Prussians would behave as they had done in 1744, that is to say retreat to the north to avoid being cut off from Breslau. To strengthen this idea he evacuated part of South-east Silesia. In truth Frederick intended to take the offensive with a force of 70,000 men as soon as the Austrian enemy could be lured down to the Silesian plain.

Prince Charles came down from the mountains on 3 June and deployed in a valley about five miles broad. Behind, on the edge of the hills, was the little town of Hohenfriedberg, and in the hills to the front of the Austrians the larger town of Striegau. The Austrian vanguard, provided by the 20,000-strong Saxon contingent under the Duke of Saxe-Weissenfels, soon made contact with a Prussian force, which it wrongly believed to be Frederick's rearguard, and it was ordered to take Striegau in the following morning. The bulk of the Prussian force lay beyond Striegau and was hidden from the enemy.

On the night of 3 June Frederick ordered forward the whole of his force across the Striegau River and, having deployed it in the dark, at first light attacked the Saxon troops on the enemy left. The Saxons were soon dislodged by the cannonade and by repeated assault of foot and horse. As a

Officer and trumpeter of hussars

soldier the Saxon was somewhat inferior to the Austrian, and usually more unlucky; but he was courageous and obstinate and, as he fought for every yard of soil, his casualties mounted alarmingly. Meanwhile Charles of Lorraine slept, and when the artillery fire awoke him he imagined it to be the Saxon attack on Striegau. He went back to sleep. When finally aroused, the battle was more than half lost and, as one chronicler said, 'the Austrians were not distinguished for celerity of movement'. The Austrian cavalry on the right wing could, and should, have been brought into action early in the engagement, but it remained passive and without orders.

Whereas the Prussian cavalry excelled itself the behaviour of the Austrian horse was surprisingly disappointing. Some Austrian regiments showed much reluctance to close with the enemy; they merely fired with their carbines, and, when the time came, ran. The Austrian infantry were shaken to pieces by the rapidity of Prussian musketry, delivered at a range of fifty paces. At eight that morning the issue had finally been decided and Charles of Lorraine ordered a retreat. Two hours later the Austrian and Saxon columns pulled back through Hohenfriedberg covered by Nadasti's rearguard. The Prussian loss had been 5,000 dead and wounded; that of the Austro-Saxons 9,000 dead and wounded, 7,000 prisoners and sixty-six cannon. A further 8,000 deserted. Frederick claimed that there had not been so great a victory since Blenheim. He did not, however, pursue the Austrians, reduced by now to 40,000, but contented himself with following up into Bohemia as far as Königgratz.

Frederick had hoped that his victory would

bring Austria and Saxony to terms. In this he was disappointed once more. Maria Theresa's determination to continue the war was shared by Augustus of Saxony, who enjoyed the encouragement and support of the Russians. Nor could England persuade Austria to make peace.

At the end of September, because he had already eaten up all the supplies in North-east Bohemia, Frederick began to fall back towards Silesia, so troubled by Nadasti's Tolpatsche that 11,000 horse and foot had to be detached to guard ration convoys. For the irregulars were quite happy to set fire to their own Queen's towns if by doing so they could deprive the Prussian. He crossed the Elbe and encamped with 18,000 men at the foot of the mountains near the village of Soor. Charles of Lorraine followed up with an army of 30,000. Then, borrowing a not very original leaf from Frederick's book, he determined to repeat the tactics of Hohenfriedberg.

On the night of 29 September nearly 30,000 Austrians, by a clever approach march in the dark, arrived on the high ground above Frederick,

A hussar trooper's arms and equipment, carbine, sabre, sabretache, ammunition-pouch and water-bottle

while a great force of pandours under Nadasti and Trenk fell on the Prussian baggage, the wild Croats murdering all in their path, women camp-followers as well as men. But the arrival of the Austrian main force was an hour too late and their movement was espied at daybreak by Prussian picquets. Frederick and his staff were already up and at work and the Prussian reactions were much quicker than those of the Austrian.

On the Austrian left wing were twenty-eight guns and fifty squadrons of horse; the guns opened fire but the horse and infantry stood immobile whereas, as Frederick said later, 'they should have thundered down on us'. When Frederick sent his cuirassiers at them, they met no countercharge, 'merely the crackle of carbines'. The Austrian cavalry wing was swept away. The Prussian foot on the right, following up the cuirassiers, climbed the slope losing heavily in the case-shot fire which raked them. The Prussians threw in their three reserve regiments of infantry. The guns were taken and the enemy driven off. Frederick then transferred the remainder of his cavalry to his left wing where the two lines still stood apart. Again the Austrian horse on that wing broke, leaving bare the infantry flank. The Austrians poured back into the forest where the Prussian cavalry could no longer pursue. Meanwhile the pandours in the rear, fully engaged in looting, brought no aid to the main battle. The engagement cost the Austrians 4,000 dead and wounded and 3,000 prisoners. The Prussian loss was about 4,000.

HENNERSDORF AND KESSELSDORF

Frederick, certain that Maria Theresa must now make peace, had returned to Berlin and his army had slowly withdrawn into Silesia, eating the country bare as it went, followed up as usual by pandours. His own army was dispersed into winter quarters and he assumed that the Austrian would do the same. The Saxons, however, had drawn up a plan to invade Brandenburg and take Berlin, and to this Maria Theresa readily agreed. Traun was to march from the Rhine while Charles made his way down the Oder. The details of the operation were blabbed, however, by the

A horse-grenadier in the so-called parade uniform which was in fact used on field service

Saxon minister Brühl, through the Swedish envoy to Berlin. The old Dessauer refused to believe it; Frederick, horrified and astonished, was finally convinced of its truth, and said that waging war on Maria Theresa 'was not living; it was being killed a thousand times a day'.

On 20 November 1745 Charles of Lorraine set out on his long march through Silesia where though the Austrians did not know it, Frederick had already arrived. The King had concentrated the Young Dessauer's forces, about 35,000 troops, near Naumburg. Three days later his forward elements, light horse, cuirassiers and foot, were in contact with the uhlans of Prince Charles's Saxon advance guard. At Hennersdorf, on 23 November, Ziethen, who was in command, destroyed the 6,000 strong Saxon force of horse and foot. Surprise having been lost, Charles turned in his tracks and retraced his steps to Bohemia. And so the whole enterprise collapsed.

Frederick now invaded Saxony. The Old Dessauer moved from Halle to Leipzig and then began a march towards Dresden, throwing a bridge over the Elbe so that Frederick, coming from Silesia, might join him. A Saxon force under Count Rutowski, together with an Austrian contingent, numbering in all 35,000, lay west of the Saxon capital. Charles of Lorraine was marching out of Bohemia with 46,000 men, in order to aid his Saxon ally. Frederick goaded on the Old Dessauer to attack the Saxons before Charles should join them, and not wait for Frederick's own arrival. When the Old Dessauer did give battle to Rutowski on 15 December, Charles of Lorraine was not five miles away.

On 15 December 1745 at Kesselsdorf the Old Dessauer attacked the entrenched Saxon force, the Prussian infantry marching uphill through wet snow against the massed fire of 9,000 muskets and thirty guns. The Prussian cavalry hung about on the outskirts. Time after time the Prussians fell back, their ranks shot through amid fearful casualties. This type of fighting suited the Saxon temperament, with time to think and time to reload. Victory would probably have been theirs had not an Austrian battalion, seeing the Prussian infantry near disintegration, left its entrenchments and, with repeated shouts of '*Sieg*', run down the slope with levelled bayonet to complete the destruction. The Saxons quickly followed and there in the valley they were cut to pieces by the Prussian horse. Rutowski lost the battle, 3,000 dead and wounded and 6,000 prisoners. The Prussians lost 4,600, but at long last gained the peace. For Charles of Lorraine turned back yet again into Bohemia.

This ended the Second Silesian War and, by the Treaty of Dresden signed on Christmas Day, Maria Theresa who had once said, and still meant, that 'she would as soon part with Silesia as with her petticoat', was forced to agree to Silesia remaining in Prussian hands. Frederick for his part acknowledged Maria Theresa's husband Francis Stephen as Emperor. Prussia, often faced with disaster, had been saved by Frederick's audacity and military skill.

The war between Austria and France continued for yet another three years in the Netherlands and Italy, peace being finally made at Aix-la-Chapelle in October 1748. The astute Maria Theresa, no less a realist than Frederick the Great, was disappointed in the terms of the peace treaty and in Britain's effort during the war. Maria Theresa knew that Britain had little interest in Silesia, the Habsburgs or Austro-Hungary and that London's only concern was to maintain the balance of power in Europe by weighing down the scales against France. She therefore began to look about her for new allies and by 1751 was already writing letters to the mistress of the French monarch, addressing her as *Madame, ma chère sœur*.

Maria Theresa's Imperial Reforms

A dragoon foot-drummer

The Treaty of Aix-la-Chapelle was regarded by Britain and France as merely a truce. Maria Theresa remained as determined as ever to regain Silesia, and her first action was to reorganize the administration and government of her own crown lands in readiness for a resumption of the struggle.

In Bohemia many Czech nobles had welcomed the Franco-Bavarian and Prussian intervention and had recognized Charles Albert, Elector of Bavaria, as the Imperial Emperor. When, two years later, the Austrians reoccupied the Bohemian kingdom, Maria Theresa resolved to eliminate all separatist tendencies. The Bohemian royal regalia was removed from Prague to Vienna to emphasize the permanency of the Austro-Czech union and the government and administration were centralized in Austrian hands. German became the language of the administration and was compulsorily taught in Czech schools; the Austrian code of law was introduced into Czech courts. This Habsburg attempt to weaken Czech nationalism and the hold of the Czech language, although understandable in the circumstances, was in fact a violation of the autonomous rights earlier guaranteed to Bohemia.

The situation in Hungary was very different. The diet, when it had met in 1741 to confirm Maria Theresa as Queen of Hungary, had offered her 100,000 Hungarian troops for use against Frederick. Only 60,000 had been forthcoming but these had conducted themselves with great dash and bravery. The nobles, however, had turned to good account the vulnerability of Austria, in securing concessions for themselves by a process akin to extortion. They insisted on a confirmation of their own freedom from taxation and their retention of appointments to key government positions in Hungary. Each concession was followed by a new demand. After the peace of 1748, Maria Theresa did not revoke these concessions made under duress but she simply declined to convoke the Hungarian diet so that the nobles would be denied the opportunity of thinking up and presenting new claims. Nor did she attempt to centralize Hungarian administration or make it conform to the Austrian pattern as she had done in Bohemia, partly in return for Hungarian loyalty and partly, as she said, 'because of the special conditions there'. Instead she tried to bind the Magyar nobility to her cause by encouraging it to enter Austrian court circles, the Austrian diplomatic service and the Austrian Army, and by conferring on it the titles and dignities of the German Empire.

Owing to the century-and-a-half occupation by the Turks, Hungary had become one of the more primitive states in Central Europe. The Hungarian diet, however, represented the interests of medieval feudalism and was a barrier between the monarchy and the Magyar people. Maria Theresa's rule was that of enlightened absolutism and she made determined efforts to improve the lot of the *jobbagy*. Serfdom was virtually eliminated in that the peasant had much of the burden of socage lifted from him, and became free to choose his own master and enter the professions. Maria Theresa did much, too, to remove education from the hands of reactionary Jesuits and hasten its growth in secular hands and, because she was decent, compassionate and charitable, set up popular elementary schools, orphanages and hospitals.

Hungary was not, however, to share the improved standard of living, even the new prosperity, of the Austrian, and the blame for this lay with the Hungarian nobility. Since Hungary declined to be taxed *per capita* on the Austrian model, the Austrian taxpayer saw little reason why he should subsidize his neighbour. Life in Hungary remained simple and backward. Both lord and peasant were hospitable and improvident; even by the not very exacting Austrian standards they were indolent.

The entire Habsburg system of government, outside Hungary, the Austrian Netherlands and Milan, was reorganized in the period between Aix-la-Chapelle and the outbreak of the Seven Years War. Maria Theresa and her minister, von Haugwitz, had been impressed by the efficiency of Frederick the Great's civil and military administration and wished to improve the Austrian. The first requirement was to raise a standing army of 108,000 men together with a military vote adequate to maintain it. Taxes were not only increased but were reorganized on a modern system of income tax, applicable to all, and a graduated poll tax; exemptions were abolished and the various diets were deprived of their former rights to levy their own taxes and duties. These new reforms trebled the Habsburg revenues so that the Austrian provinces in Germany and Bohemia were soon shouldering over three quarters of the cost of the new military expenditure. Much was done, too, to extend industrialization and education in the Austrian homeland and restrict the hitherto inviolable hereditary rights of the noble and great landowner. The great improvement in Austrian military efficiency during the Seven Years War was largely due to von Haugwitz.

The Seven Years War

With the assistance of the Austrian Chancellor, Count von Kaunitz-Reitberg, Maria Theresa at last succeeded in breaking the Franco-Prussian alliance. The English King, George II of Hanover, would have welcomed a renewal of the Anglo-Austrian agreement in order to safeguard Hanover against Prussia. Vienna was little interested, so London turned to St. Petersburg where, in exchange for a subsidy, the Empress Elisabeth promised to mass a Russian force of 55,000 against the Prussian border. Frederick the Great was placed in a difficult situation. Fearing the Russian, so he said, more than he feared God, and being aware that Elisabeth and her minister, Count Bestuzhev-Ryumin, were bitterly anti-Prussian, he had good reason to expect a joint Austro-Russian attack on East Prussia and Silesia.

An officer of cuirassiers together with a trooper in stable fatigue dress

In this event France was too far away to afford him direct and speedy assistance. In order to neutralize Russia, he turned to Britain and by the Convention of Westminster, signed in January 1756, agreed to ensure the neutrality of Germany on the understanding that London would drop the Russian pact; this was some safeguard to Hanover. Elisabeth of Russia, annoyed at the British action, offered Austria an alliance, undertaking to attack Prussia if the alliance were accepted. This set off a further diplomatic reaction in that France, unwilling to be isolated on the continent of Europe and angry at Frederick's new convention with the British, entered into a defensive alliance with Austria.

The loser was Frederick. His insulting raillery had made enemies of the French king and Russian empress and his attempt to neutralize the Anglo-Russian threat had drawn Russia, Austria and France in league against him. Russia, Austria and Saxony were openly hostile to Prussia. But he had a standing army of 150,000 men and 14,000,000 thalers put aside for war. He, therefore, without warning and without consulting Britain, attacked Austria in September 1756 by invading Saxony, thus setting loose a new continental war.

The Seven Years War, sometimes known as the Third Silesian War, was a resumption of the struggle for the retention of Silesia and the mastery of the German Empire. Moreover for Frederick it was a war of survival for, if Prussia failed, it would be dismembered by the powerful coalition which faced it.

Although heavily outnumbered, Rutowski and 18,000 Saxon troops entrenched in mountainous Pirna put up an unexpectedly tough resistance, gaining time for Austria to mobilize; Frederick besieged but declined to attack them. Field-Marshal Browne was sent to relieve the besieged Saxons but met with Frederick's forces on 1 October 1756 at Lobositz. The Prussians were somewhat shaken by the much improved quality of the Austrian infantry and artillery, and by the new efficiency in tactical command. Browne was on the ground first but failed to take the pass, an error which he partially retrieved on the day of the battle. For he put the Austrian horse out as a bait which twenty squadrons of Prussian cavalry

Charge of the Austrian Dragoons at the Battle of Kolin 1757, where the Prussians under Frederick the Great were totally defeated. From a painting by Koch.

1 Artillery Fusilier, summer field
service uniform, c. 1751
2 Artilleryman (Kanonier), winter
field service uniform, c. 1740
3 Gunner (Büchsenmeister) of Artillery,
summer field service uniform, c. 1751

R. OTTENFELD

A

Horse-Grenadier,
winter parade uniform, c. 1750

B

R. OTTENFELD

1 **Officer of German Infantry,**
  summer field service uniform, c. 1750
2 **Dragoon, summer field**
  service order, c. 1750
3 **Hungarian Infantry Soldier,**
  summer field service uniform, c. 1756

R. OTTENFELD

C

Hussar, winter field
service uniform, c. 1743

D

R. OTTENFELD

1 Soldier of Frontier Infantry,
  summer field service uniform, c. 1750
2 Sharpshooter (Scharfschütz) of Frontier
  Infantry, summer patrol uniform c. 1750
3 Cuirassier, summer field
  service order, c. 1750

R. OTTENFELD

E

I

2

Trenk'scher Pandour and
Carlstädter Sluiner Croat, c. 1756

R. OTTENFELD

1 General of Cavalry,
  winter parade uniform, c. 1760
2 Engineer Officer,
  winter field service uniform, c. 1760
3 Private Soldier of Sappers,
  winter field service uniform, c. 1760

R. OTTENFELD

G

1 Fifer of German Infantry,
  summer field service uniform, c. 1769
2 Private Soldier of Hungarian Infantry,
  summer field service uniform, c. 1770
3 Fusilier of German Infantry,
  summer field service uniform, c. 1769

H

R. OTTENFELD

greedily took, chasing off the Austrians helter-skelter; they were drawn almost into the muzzles of hidden Austrian batteries which mowed them down with case-shot. After this unpromising start Frederick ordered his infantry, loaded with ninety cartridges a man, to take Lobositz.

Fighting was particularly fierce and the Austrian infantry, now equipped with iron instead of wooden ramrods, were most determined, returning to the Prussian volley for volley. Browne's flank broke, but he moved with haste and skill and soon recovered. After seven hours of fighting the Prussians, though they had suffered more casualties, 3,300 against the Austrian 2,900, still barred the way to Pirna.

Maria Theresa ordered Browne 'to deliver me these poor Saxons at any price'. Browne's final attempt, enterprising though it was, failed because the Saxons, much reduced by hunger, were too weak to carry out their allotted part of the operation. Rutowski capitulated. All Saxon officers were dismissed and the Saxon rank and file were forcibly incorporated into the Prussian army, with Prussian officers and uniform. Saxony itself remained in Prussian occupation for nearly six years.

Yet Frederick had made a poor beginning to the war. The German Protestant rulers were, admittedly, generally sympathetic to him but, in face of Austrian diplomacy, his position was rapidly deteriorating. Russia agreed to enter the war against him in return for an Austrian subsidy. Maria Theresa offered to trade the Austrian Netherlands to France and Spain in exchange for active participation in the war and the return of Silesia to Austria. Sweden entered the war against Prussia.

Austria Victorious

The Prussian outposts were much troubled by pandours of all nationalities, Hungarians, Croats and Poles, most wearing a uniform of a sort, devised by their leaders and improved upon by the wearers. These so-called Frei Korps usually took the names of cavalry or pandour leaders such as Trenck, Nadasti, or the Scot, Loudon.

Frederick's answer to any political or military threat was to attack. In the spring of 1757 he invaded Bohemia with four columns, three from Saxony and the fourth, under Schwerin, from Silesia. There 133,000 Austrians were making ready to cross into Silesia. Maria Theresa had once more given the overall Austrian command to her inexperienced brother-in-law, Charles of Lorraine. As the Prussians advanced Charles fell back with 60,000 men to the neighbourhood of Prague to await the arrival of a further 30,000 Austrians under Field-Marshal Daun. Frederick was determined to rout Charles before Daun should join him and, against Schwerin's wishes and advice, he ordered the 64,000 tired Prussians to attack the entrenched positions east of the Bohemian capital. For Frederick had become overweeningly confident in his own superiority and in what he believed to be the invincibility of his troops. Time was pressing and Daun was not ten miles away.

On 6 May 1757 Frederick was at the pinnacle of his fame. He had just joined with Schwerin outside Prague and together they reconnoitred the outskirts of the Austrian position. They reckoned this to be so strong that they decided to outflank it by marching round the enemy right to his rear, there to attack across what they imagined to be green meadows. These lush fields were in fact carp ponds, two to three feet deep, covered with water weed. The circuitous march was conducted with skill, but the Prussians were disconcerted to see the Austrians, under the energetic leadership of Browne, counter without any hesitation by immediately changing front at the double. When the Prussian infantry arrived at the carp ponds they were met by the tearing fire of artillery case-shot at 400 paces. They stormed the batteries, however, but were then thrown out again by Austrian grenadiers. To and fro the battle raged for hours, the seventy-three-year-old Schwerin, a veteran of Blenheim, being killed by grape as he rallied broken regiments. Browne, too, directing the Austrian defence at this spot, was mortally wounded.

The Austrian horse had already been chased

from the field but the infantry fought like lions, every surviving grenadier henceforth getting double pay for life. Yet the battle ended with the Prussians in possession of the field, the Austrians having been forced back into Prague. But the King himself had been most unpleasantly surprised; 'these are not by any means the old Austrians' he wrote very mournfully, 'this day saw the pillars of the Prussian infantry cut down'. He doubted whether he could ever replace the quality of his losses. Prussia certainly lost at least 13,000 men that day, the same number as the Austrians, but the King had earlier put his own loss at 18,000. The battle was heralded abroad among Prussia's allies as a great victory for Frederick, and the Tower of London guns fired a salute. The Prussians had, admittedly, captured much equipment; on the other hand, Charles of Lorraine's army, 46,000 strong, was still in being, although besieged in Prague. Daun, not far away, had been further reinforced and, having collected up and reformed the stragglers of the Prague battle, had now 60,000 men under his command.

Daun was very cautious, known even among the Austrians as a 'Fabius Cunctator'. One brave heart in Vienna was still not dismayed, for Maria Theresa entreated him to give battle, assuring him that even if he were defeated he would still enjoy the royal favour. The choice was already out of Daun's hands, however, for Frederick, having unsuccessfully besieged Prague for a month, was on the march in search of the Austrian field-marshal.

Although Daun lacked dash and initiative, he was experienced and clever in defence. He had taken up a strong position parallel to the Vienna-Prague highway not far from Kolin. While Frederick, only three miles away, remained in ignorance of where the Austrians were to be found, Daun was well informed of the Prussian activity by the pandours.

About 30,000 Prussians moved in march route along the highway towards Kolin on 18 June, to find the route blocked by a large force of Austrian horse under Nadasti. These were soon driven off by Ziethen's Prussian cavalry. Frederick, re-

Mounted and dismounted pandour irregulars, c. 1750

garding Daun's entrenched position on the slopes to the right of the road as impregnable, decided to outflank it by marching along the Austrian front and round the enemy right, exactly as he had done at Prague. On this day, however, nothing went right. Ziethen's force, galloping after enemy cavalry and foot, ran into a trap and was taken in the flank by artillery and infantry, cleverly concealed in oak woods and copses. Thereafter Ziethen remained separated from the main battle. The Prussian infantry trying to get round the Austrian right flank were soon pinned by enemy fire and counter-attacks. The following up Prussian columns, still in march formation, were drawn, willy nilly, into the frontal battle on ground of Daun's choosing. The Prussian centre was said to be wrongly directed (although this did not come to light until many years afterwards) by Frederick himself, in the heat of battle, mistaking left for right. For the consequent disorder the Prussian General Mannstein got much of the blame, since his troops, angry at their rising casualties caused by the fire of Hungarian and Croat skirmishers hidden in the corn and scrub, turned off the allotted march route to deal with them. Mannstein, badly wounded himself, was unable to make his excuses since he was murdered several days later by pandours who waylaid his carriage.

So the battle was joined along the whole of the Austrian front, raging indecisively for hours. Daun began to fear that he would be forced off the high ground into the swamp behind, and sent out messages in case a withdrawal should be needed. These were received by his subordinates with indignation. Some Austrian horse, including Nostitz's Saxon cavalry brigade and de Thiennes Netherland Walloon regiment of dragoons, held back in reserve without seeing any action that day, asked that they might be permitted at least to strike a blow. Daun agreed 'if they thought it would be any use'. A force was hastily improvised including supporting infantry and guns, and this Austrian cavalry decided the day. Frederick quitted the field, and the Prussians were already in rapid retreat, harried by the Austrian General Sampach. Daun did not pursue further, although the Prussian was by then thoroughly beaten, for as one historian said 'as a good Christian, he did not like the sun to go down on his wrath'. The total Austrian loss, including wounded, was 8,000; the Prussians lost 8,000 dead and nearly another 6,000 prisoners, forty-five cannon and much equipment. The main casualties were caused to the flower of the Prussian infantry.

Thereafter fortune deserted Frederick for, as he himself admitted, he had been decisively defeated at Kolin. He had to quit Bohemia. Britain, too, found little consolation in its new choice of ally, since Frederick was powerless to prevent the French occupation of Hanover. In the second half of 1757 the Swedes invaded Prussian Pomerania while the Russians defeated a Prussian force at Gross-Jagerndorf in East Prussia. Maria Theresa's forces spilled over into Silesia and an Austrian cavalry and partisan force under General Haddik, 15,000 strong, raided Berlin and extracted from the capital a ransom of a quarter of a million thalers.

The Prussian Recovery

Frederick survived the summer and autumn of 1757 because of the lack of coordination between his enemies. The Russians, believing that the Empress Elisabeth was dead, withdrew out of East Prussia, while the French force in Hanover remained inactive. In Lusatia, Daun and Prince Charles had outmanoeuvred a Prussian force under the King's brother Augustus William but, in spite of Maria Theresa's urging, they would not come to grips with the enemy. In November a French army under Soubise began to move through Thuringia on Saxony, joining up with some Saxons and an Austrian force under Hildburghausen. In all the Franco-Austrian force numbered 50,000 men.

The French were contemptuous of Prussian arms. When the Prussian force first approached the Franco-Austrian positions near Rossbach, and then rapidly withdrew as soon as engaged by artillery fire (the position being very strong and little to Frederick's liking), Soubise became obsessed with the idea that Frederick was in full retreat and might escape him. Believing that the Prussians had only 10,000 men (in reality they had more than twice that number), Soubise set off in immediate pursuit, intending to outflank and get across the Prussian line of withdrawal. The truth was much otherwise. For Frederick himself entertained the same mistaken thoughts about his enemy, who he knew to be short of rations, and he believed the French were about to run away. Having halted in some dead ground and sat down to his dinner, he was astonished when his hussars reported that the enemy was streaming by on the other side of the hill in column of route, the trotting cavalry in front leaving the panting infantry far behind.

It was already well past noon that winter's day, but within half an hour the Prussians were deployed to attack the moving enemy in the flank. Thirty-eight squadrons, about 4,000 horse, under Seydlitz hit the surprised enemy column, and infantry and guns followed. By four o'clock the Franco-Austrian force was in flight leaving 3,000 dead and wounded and 5,000 prisoners, of whom eight were generals and 300 officers. The Prussians lost 500 dead and wounded, and not half of their strength had come into action; Seydlitz's horse and seven battalions had done all the work. Thus ended the battle of Rossbach.

The days of the Dessauers were nearly over and Schwerin and Winterfeld were no more. The only Prussian general of outstanding distinction, besides Frederick, was Ferdinand of Brunswick and he was now in command of the Anglo-

German infantry in parade order. The mounted figure in the centre is a major, the officer to the right a colonel wearing dismounted-pattern gaiters. Dismounted officers carried pikes as a badge of office and as protection against cavalry

German force in Hanover. Charles of Lorraine had begun to inflict a series of defeats on the Prussian generals. He had taken Breslau. The Prussian Bevern was captured by Croat irregulars and his army fled to Glogau. The Saxon and Silesian troops in Prussian service were deserting Frederick *en masse*. Silesia was about to fall from the Prussian grasp when, at the end of November, Frederick arrived at the head of only 14,000 weary men. The command of Bevern's remnants, about 18,000, he gave to Ziethen.

Frederick was determined to attack, whatever the odds, though it is doubtful whether he knew that Charles of Lorraine and Traun, now joined by Nadasti, had 80,000 men drawn up at Leuthen. The Austrian position, however, was not a strong one, being overextended and nearly seven miles in length. Its observation was masked by a ridge to its front, and this was held only by a Saxon brigade of horse and two Austrian hussar regiments. The ridge was soon cleared by the Prussians, the Saxon General Nostitz being killed in the encounter.

In the main Austrian line, the Italian General Lucchesi commanded the right and Nadasti the left, with Traun in the centre. Lucchesi was convinced that his right would be attacked and in response to his entreaties was eventually heavily reinforced; in fact Frederick attacked the left, moving in on it in his new oblique order. There the Croats and Würtemburgers eventually broke; and when Lucchesi led a cavalry charge from the right of the field to the left, in support of the faltering left wing, he was himself taken in the flank by hidden Prussian horse, routed, and killed.

Yet Charles and Daun acted with greater celerity than they had ever done before, throwing men over from right to left into the village of Leuthen, where the church and churchyard were bitterly defended. But the far-flung positions cost them both time and the battle, for the men, arriving piecemeal, were blown before they struck a blow. Three times the Austrians attempted to rally and stand, only to be swept from the field. Leuthen, probably the greatest of all Prussian victories, cost the Austrians 3,000 dead, 7,000 wounded, 21,000 prisoners and 116 guns lost. The total Prussian loss was under 7,000.

The defeat lost Charles of Lorraine his post as Commander-in-Chief, henceforth assumed by Daun.

The Final Stages

The French had been driven across the Rhine and, after Leuthen, most of Silesia was reconquered by the Prussians. The British took advantage of Frederick's successes to reoccupy Hanover.

In the spring of 1758 a new Prussian army moved through Moravia to Olmütz on its way to Vienna only to lose its heavily guarded supply train of 4,000 wagons to General Loudon, said to be the best partisan leader of the times. Frederick withdrew once more through Bohemia into Silesia. Meanwhile the Russians, back again in East Prussia, moved on Brandenburg only to be repulsed at Zorndorf in August in one of the bloodiest battles of the war.

The indomitable Austrians had raised two more armies. One they dispatched to Saxony and the other to Silesia. That October, the first of these armies, under Daun, defeated Frederick at Hochkirch near Bautzen. Frederick had encamped his 30,000 men in an untenable position facing Daun's 60,000, and he met the protests of his own Prussian generals 'that in such a situation Daun ought to be hung if he did not attack', with the arrogant retort 'that the Austrians fear us more than the gallows'. Daun did attack, however, before daylight and, although he lost 6,000 Austrians, he destroyed a quarter of Frederick's force. This was the third of Daun's victories over the King in sixteen months. Once more he failed to follow up his advantage, the Austrian neglect permitting Frederick to keep his forces intact and outmanoeuvre his foes.

By early 1759 the Prussian field army had been reduced to 100,000 men, many of them recruits, and in August of that year a large Russian force under Saltykov, already in Frankfurt-on-Oder, defeated, with some Austrian support, the Prussians at Kunersdorf. The Russians refused to pursue since they believed that the Grand Duke Peter, an admirer of Frederick the Great, was about to ascend the Russian throne. Saltykov spent his time in debauchery. Meanwhile the Austrians remained in Saxony, manoeuvring and counter-manoeuvring. In November Frederick returned to his armies there and this was the signal for Daun to withdraw. The sneering King sent Finck and 15,000 Prussians to pursue; Frederick lost every single man when Daun turned on Finck's army and encircled it. On 21 November 1759 the Prussians laid down their arms at Maxen.

The French, however, were still doing badly. They had been defeated at Minden by an Anglo-German force and had suffered serious military defeats overseas. By 1759 they had reduced the subsidy to Maria Theresa and were no longer interested even in the Austrian Netherlands as the price of restoring Silesia to Austria. France was rapidly dropping out of the European war.

The year 1760 was the last year of the great campaigns. The Austrians sent a further army into Silesia. Loudon, the aggressive Scot, an experienced field commander as well as partisan leader, drove the Prussian force under Fouqué

A front view of the ubiquitous three pounder field gun

out of Landshut. Frederick indignantly ordered the place to be retaken. Like Finck, Fouqué obeyed his master's order to the letter and failed. For Loudon destroyed his 10,000-strong army, only 1,500 Prussian cavalry escaping.

Frederick was having no better fortune against the two Austrians, Daun and Lacy, in Saxony. He besieged Dresden but failed to take it. Then, hearing the bad news from the east, he set out yet again for Silesia, with Daun and Lacy hanging on his flanks. When they arrived in Silesia Daun joined up with Loudon, outnumbering the Prussian force of 30,000 by nearly three to one, and barring Frederick's path at Liegnitz. Frederick was in a desperate position. He was short of rations and had a string of defeats behind him; a large Russian army stood across the Oder waiting the outcome of Daun's battle and had already thrown bridges across the water; the fighting efficiency of the Austrian soldier was greatly superior to that of the first two Silesian Wars and, whereas the Prussian recruit was in decline, the Austro-Hungarian material was still improving.

On 14 August Frederick was several miles to the south-west of Liegnitz while Daun and Loudon lay ten miles to the north-east of the town. Hearing from an Austrian deserter that the enemy intended to make a night approach that very evening to attack his camp before first light, the Prussian army moved immediately after darkness several miles towards the enemy and lay down on some high ground near the village of Panten, right astride the Austrian approach route. The first to come up the hill was Loudon's force, out of touch with Daun, Loudon himself leading with no advance guard deployed. On being challenged the Austrians attacked. At first they thought they had brushed a Prussian baggage train, but when the truth became known, Loudon, undeterred, threw in his whole force with such dash and momentum that the Prussian left was well-nigh cut in two. The fighting lasted an hour and a half, the Prussians rallied and drove out the Austrians with a loss, so they claimed, of 6,000 dead and wounded and 4,000 prisoners. Loudon had lost a third of his force and fell back unsupported, since Daun was still too far away to do anything but engage the Prussian right. Daun, in spite of the Empress's urging, declined to attack once more.

An officer of Hungarian infantry

Nor did the Russians across the Oder care to take up the engagement, notwithstanding their superiority in numbers. Yet Frederick did not dare to delay on the field of battle and, only four hours afterwards at nine o'clock in the morning of 15 August, he was already away, having cleared the field of guns, muskets and wounded, both Prussian and Austrian.

Loudon was censured by some for his impetuousity. Yet the issue was so close that Frederick himself said that if the attack had been made only a quarter of an hour earlier, it would have gone badly with the Prussians.

At the beginning of October a Russian raiding force of 20,000 tried to take Berlin but failed. A week later 15,000 Austrian troops under Lacy joined them and the capital was occupied for a few days, the inhabitants paying a ransom of four million thalers. The raiding force, hearing that Frederick was approaching, then withdrew, Lacy moving off to Saxony.

In Saxony was fought the last great battle of the war, for Frederick had returned to his main recruiting ground and treasure-house. Daun had followed, to be joined by Lacy. The master of defence had entrenched himself near the Elbe at Torgau with 50,000 troops; Frederick with 44,000, was determined to attack him. Making over a third of his force to Ziethen, who had, however, no experience of higher field command, he ordered him to attack frontally on the Austrian right flank. Frederick, with the main body, made a long circuitous march of fourteen miles through the forest and attacked Daun from the rear.

Daun had 400 guns, a half of them new, and these, quickly redeploying, did fearful execution among Frederick's attacking infantry. The battle had started at about midday and was of the fiercest, but because of some confusion Ziethen's frontal attack did not materialize; by early evening the Austrians had the best of it so that the wounded Daun sent a messenger off to Vienna announcing a victory. This was Frederick's view, too, for he had withdrawn for the night, some miles away, intending to renew the attack the next day. At six in the evening in pitch darkness Ziethen's force, over five hours late, came into serious action for the first time at the place appointed for its attack to the Austrian front. Hülsen, in command of Frederick's bivouaced forces, called them to arms again and went in to attack the rear. In a few hours the battle was lost to Daun. Torgau was his last great battle, as it was Frederick's. Frederick was later to say it was the severest and most crucial battle of the war. The Prussians lost 14,000 men against an Austrian loss of 20,000 and 45 guns. Daun's army remained, however, still in being, and still ready for battle.

Finale

The strain of the war was telling not only against Prussia, which with a population of under five million was keeping an army in the field which rarely fell in strength below 100,000, but also against the French and Austro-Russian coalition, which with a population of a hundred million had nearly a quarter of a million troops in Western and Central Europe. Kaunitz warned Maria Theresa in December 1760 that Austria had resources left for only one more campaign; in the following spring the Austrian forces were reduced by 20,000 men.

Britain's new monarch, George III, wanted an end to the war and this was a widely shared feeling in Britain and France; overseas, Britain had done well and France badly, and by 1762 the British subsidy to Prussia was no longer paid. In January 1762, however, the European situation was entirely changed by the death of the Tsarina Elisabeth. Her successor, the Grand Duke Peter, was a German whose principal interest appeared to be centred in the Duchy of Oldenburg and in a dynastic claim against Denmark for Schleswig-Holstein. Moreover Peter admired Frederick the Great and mistrusted Austria. So he withdrew from the war and concluded an alliance with Prussia directed at both Austria and Denmark.

Sweden also made peace. The murder of Peter some months later did not alter the political situation in that the new monarch in St. Petersburg, Catherine the Great, while having no intention of intervening on Frederick's behalf, merely confirmed the peace made by her predecessor. She ordered all Russian troops from Germany.

Maria Theresa was now isolated and in July and October 1762 Frederick won two further victories when he began to clear Silesia of Austrian troops. Realizing that she could no longer hope unaided to win and keep Silesia she came to terms with Frederick. Frederick refused to accept the mediation of Britain and France, stating his own terms of 'not a foot of land and no compensation to Saxony, not a village, not a penny'. He agreed to evacuate Saxony but held Silesia. The Treaty of Hubertusburg of February 1763 between Prussia and Austria made no alterations to the frontiers of Europe; and so 'a million men had perished but not a hamlet had changed its ruler'.

A soldier carpenter, probably of a grenadier unit

AUSTRO-HUNGARIAN ARMY UNIFORM

In spite of Maria Theresa's efforts to enforce regulations, the Austro-Hungarian Army dress of the period was hardly uniform, for there was a general lack of orders on the subject and the appearance of regiments depended largely on the money and stocks of materials available, the tastes of the colonels, the standard of discipline, and, finally, on the wearer himself. Hussar officers might, admittedly, devise their own undress or off-parade uniform by shedding the dolman and donning a tricorne. Some of the cavalry too had a fatigue stable dress. But most troops had only one pattern of uniform, and this served both as parade dress and for field service. And the difference between summer and winter field service uniform was simply a matter of with or without greatcoat.

The Plates

A1 Artillery Fusilier, summer field service uniform, c. 1751

The artillery fusilier wore the distinctive artillery uniform of the period except for the infantry-pattern button-up gaiters, and he was armed with the usual infantry short sabre together with a musket and bayonet, his primary task being to give close infantry protection to the guns. Fusiliers had been raised initially because infantry commanders objected to the whittling away of their fighting strength by detaching men to the artillery. In 1757 fusilier companies were grouped into artillery fusilier regiments, a regiment having three battalions, each of eight companies of 116 men. In addition to his protective role, the fusilier could also perform the duties of the Handlanger-dienst, a pool of artillery labour which dug gun emplacements and fortifications, moved the guns into action and assisted with ammunition supply. After Hubertusburg the fusiliers were reduced to one regiment and finally disbanded in 1772.

A2 Artilleryman (Kanonier), winter field service uniform c. 1740

Austria entered the First Silesian War with virtually the same artillery as it had used at Blenheim. In 1740 all artillerymen wore the pearl-grey uniform with ponceau-rot facings, together with the black-and-gold-ribboned three-cornered hat which, incidentally, was common at this time to artillerymen of other continental armies. The brown uniforms were introduced later. Officers continued to wear the red waistcoat. All artillery, except for horse parties, were clean shaven, and gunners were allowed to wear side locks not more than 16 cm. in length. Officers wore a pigtail, either a short thick Zopf known as the 'cannon' or the long thin Rattenschwanz. Unter-kanoniere and their corporals were armed with an infantry musket and cartridge-pouch, but the Kanonier carried pike and sword and wore a leather case (Besteck) for his tools, slung over one shoulder. Until 1770 there were more three-pounder guns in the Austrian artillery than any

other piece, and this particular plate is of interest in that it shows the detail of gun, equipment, chocks, ramrod, charge-rod and linch-pins. The gunner's pike (Luntenstock) was originally designed for the number one or gunlayer to touch off the charge with the heated tip, but by 1740 the pike had become both a ceremonial badge of office and a weapon of defence to ward off attacking cavalry.

A3 Gunner (Büchsenmeister) of Artillery, summer field service uniform, c. 1751

The acknowledged founder of Austrian gunnery was Joseph Wenzel, Prince of Lichtenstein, for when he took over responsibility for the artillery it had only 800 gunners. Its size soon increased, however, so that by 1755, when the corps of artillery really came into being, it had three brigades, each of eight companies, and thirty-three independent field and fortress companies. An artillery brigade was the equivalent of a regiment commanded by a colonel, with a lieutenant-colonel and two Obristwachtmeister (majors) as staff. A company was commanded by a captain and consisted of seventy men. Within the artillery, but with an entirely separate corporate existence, were the bombardiers who manned the howitzers and mortars. The chief bombardier (Ober-feuerwerksmeister) was usually responsible for all higher gunnery training. The artillery uniform colour at this particular time was brown with poppy-coloured (*ponceau-rot*) facings and linings, together with the black three-cornered hat trimmed with gold lace. The weapon common to all gunners was the short infantry-pattern sabre. The Büchsenmeister was a first-class gunner who commanded one or more gun crews but he was not a master-gunner in the English sense of the term.

B Horse-Grenadier, winter parade uniform, c. 1750

The foot grenadier was originally a grenade-thrower, but when the function was extended to the cavalry, the designation of horse-grenadier proved to be a misnomer since it was virtually impossible for a mounted man to throw a grenade any distance, and dragoons were already trained in dismounted grenade-throwing. However, the Austrian forces, like those of the other continental powers, introduced horse-grenadiers, who soon became light-horse or carabiniers, and a few decades later the light horse and dragoons were temporarily amalgamated to form light dragoons. Cuirassiers, dragoons and light horse, when mounted, carried the musket or carbine on a broad shoulder-belt, muzzle upwards as shown in this plate. At about this time a cavalry commission recommended that the carbine and musket of hussars and light cavalry should be carried in the fashion of other armies, suspended from the swivel muzzle down, since this enabled the soldier to fire quickly from the saddle. The results were unfortunate in that the firing mechanism and lock were often damaged by the jolting, and the ball fell out of the loaded barrel. Other recommendations of the commission were more pertinent, particularly the abolition of the stiff leather boot-linings (known as Faschinen). For though they improved the look of the boot they were a danger to the soldier since they prevented him from running. The green coat shown here became traditional for light horse.

C1 Officer of German Infantry, summer field service uniform, c. 1750

In 1757, at the end of the Third Silesian War, there were fifty-seven regular infantry regiments in Maria Theresa's army, of which forty-six were German. There had been great difficulty in compelling the colonels to conform to the dress regulations, but eventually all regular German infantry adopted the white half-length coat and breeches. There was some variation, according to regiment, in the colours of the waistcoat (kamisol) and the coat-linings and facings. The number and the position of buttons were at the regiment's discretion, except that they were to be of the standard brass metal issue. The blue of the facings and lining shown in this plate indicate that the officer probably came from the Baden Durlach Regiment (later 27 Infantry Regiment), and his boots and spurs show that he was a major or colonel, for company officers usually wore a white spat form of gaiter. Rank badges were not taken into general use until 1765, when epaulettes and Achselschlingen were issued for all officer ranks

Sappers in action breaking down a church wall, c. 1762

from colonel to Fahnencadett.

C2 Dragoon, summer field service order, c. 1750

It was Maria Theresa's wish that cuirassier regiments should gradually be converted to wearing white coats with red facings while dragoons should wear the white tunic (Rock) with blue facings, as shown on this plate. She was in fact unsuccessful, partly because of the intervention of the many wars, but principally because of the conservatism within the regiments. For the colonels regarded regiments almost as their own property, even to the extent of putting their own heraldic devices on the shabracks instead of the imperial double-eagle. And so the Latour and Walloon Dragoons continued to wear their historic Netherland green, while the Savoy Dragoons kept their red and blue; few regiments did in fact convert to the white, and those that did, such as the Althan and the Wallachian Dragoons, took scarlet instead of blue facings. The dragoon could fight as a cavalryman but he owed his origin to mounted infantry, and carried a bayonet as well as a sword; his musket was five inches longer than the cuirassier's carbine.

C3 Hungarian Infantry Soldier, summer field service uniform, c. 1756

When Maria Theresa came to the throne there were only three regular Hungarian infantry regiments forming part of the Austro-Hungarian armed forces. The Queen was popular in Hungary and recruiting was successful for the 1741 war, yet only eight new Hungarian infantry regiments were raised. This was considerably short of the anticipated number, but difficulties arose since few Magyar recruits, however enthusiastic they might be, wanted to be infantrymen. In accordance with the national temperament all wanted to be hussars, or, if they could not be cavalry, then they preferred to join the Frei Korps or irregulars. Because it was below Hungarian dignity to march, the infantry enrolled were hardly to be compared to the quality of the German regiments. The Hungarian lacked the mentality to stick at laborious and monotonous routine and he found discipline irksome; according to the Austrian account, some Magyar infantry deserted at the time of the siege of Prague 'because

A cuirassier's saddlery, broadsword and carbine (until 1769)

a cold rain had fallen throughout the previous night'. Hungarian efficiency much improved, however, under the stricter discipline enforced by Khevenhüller. In the year 1746 the white coat was taken into use by Hungarian infantry, usually with blue facings on the sleeve and the back of the collar and up to 1756 waistcoats and trousers were of different regimental colours; thereafter most were changed to blue as in this plate.

D Hussar, winter field service uniform, c. 1743

Hussars first entered the Austrian service by way of Hungary, where they had been used in the southern frontier areas as light horsemen. The hussar had many functions for, although he was used as a line cavalryman, he specialized in scouting and outpost duty, in denying the enemy reconnaissance and in long-range raiding. He was armed with a carbine, usually carried at his right side suspended by a broad shoulder-strap, a pair of pistols and a sabre, here shown hanging from his wrist by the sword-knot. He never carried a lance. His distinctive fur headdress with hanging bag, dolman, boots, facings and accoutrements were adopted by the hussars of other nations.

E1 Soldier of Frontier Infantry, summer field service uniform, c. 1750

Frontier infantry regiments had some specialized training in patrol work but they were primarily intended to repel or take the first shock of invading forces; in consequence they were equipped and trained as line infantry. Like the line, they used the general service (ordinär) infantry flintlock musket, first designed in 1722, with a barrel of 18·3 mm. bore, a length of 157 cm. and a weight of 4·8 kg. Its stock and butt were of beech. This musket, which remained in service until after 1754, could deliver up to three rounds a minute when fired by a trained soldier using a paper con- container cartridge. Fire was usually by volley, the grand volley (Salvenfeuer), or by Gassen-, Hohlweg-, Hecken-, and Bachfeuer, the type of fire not being related to the ground but only to the deployment formation of the troops. An in- fantry line was usually in fours, after 1756 in threes. The bayonet was intended primarily for defence against cavalry, and although infantry could and did use it on occasion in close-quarter fighting, German infantry usually used the butt of the musket as a club, while the Hungarian was taught to rely on the sabre. All frontier infantry wore white trousers, but the colour of the coat could be white, brown or *wolfsgrau*.

E2 Sharpshooter (Scharfschütz) of Frontier Infantry,
   summer patrol uniform, c. 1750
The border sharpshooters formed a reinforced company 256 strong in each frontier regiment, and they were in fact snipers and light infantry, expert in patrolling, observation and the provision of screens. In training and marksmanship they were reckoned to be vastly superior to the regular infantry of the line. Sharpshooters were equipped with a variety of weapons, according to their tasks, including high velocity air-guns and rifles.

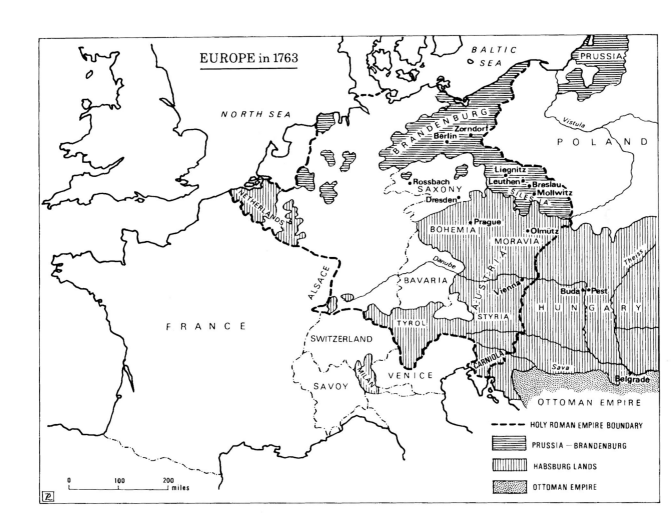

EUROPE in 1763

HOLY ROMAN EMPIRE BOUNDARY
PRUSSIA — BRANDENBURG
HABSBURG LANDS
OTTOMAN EMPIRE

The usual weapon, however, was a double-barrelled carbine, the upper barrel being rifled and the lower a smooth bore; forty paper cartridges were carried on each man for the smooth, and seventy ball for the rifled (the powder for the latter being kept in a powder-horn). These expensive weapons were often carried in a protective leather case, slung over the shoulder. The pike served both to protect the soldier from cavalry and as a rifle support when shooting; in addition the sharpshooter carried a Hungarian sabre but no bayonet.

E3 Cuirassier, summer field service order, c. 1750
In spite of the unauthorized variation and indiscipline in dress, cuirassier regiments were probably more uniform and stricter in detail than any other horse. The cuirassier's three-cornered hat was always black with a black cockade, and usually without coloured edging; his coat was white and neckerchief black. Facings were usually red, as were pantaloons, although in one of the eighteen cuirassier regiments (the Modena), pantaloons were blue, and in four others (Stampach, Albert von Sachsen, Brettlach, Anhalt-Zerbst) they were yellow. There was some minor variation in the colour of waistcoats. The heavy broadsword (Pallasch) had a leather scabbard with the metal scabbard-furnishings, guard and hilt of the same colour as the buttons. The trooper carried a pair of pistols and a short carbine and wore the armoured cuirass. When fighting against the Turks the cuirassier used additional body armour and a casque.

F Trenk'scher Pandour and Carlstädter Sluiner Croat, c. 1756
Trenck was born in Calabria in 1711 as the son of a colonel in the Austrian service, a baron originally from Prussia. He joined the Hungarian infantry regiment Leopold Palffy as a Fähnrich, retiring as a lieutenant to his estate at Brestovac. After serving in the Frei Korps in Bosnia he entered the Russian service from which he retired with the rank of major. He then set up his own robber band and soon fell foul of the law, fleeing to Vienna and taking sanctuary in a monastery. From there he was extricated by Charles of Lorraine, through whom Trenck gained an

A cuirassier on guard duty, c. 1750

audience with Maria Theresa. Recommissioned as an Obristwachtmeister he was given authority to raise volunteers in the Danube-Save area to the south. The nature of the leader was such that he attracted to his ranks a bloodthirsty band of cutthroats and looters. Recruits received only six Kreuzer a day, a Kreuzer being worth about a penny, unless they were in rations when they got less; they had no officer corps but merely a 'harumbasha' in charge of each party of fifty men (and he, too, received no more than the statutory six Kreuzer). Although they were brought to Vienna and given a uniform of sorts, so that Maria Theresa could review them, in fact they wore what they pleased; the only uniformity among them was that they shaved their heads, leaving only a topknot of hair rather like a pig-tail. Yet from a military viewpoint their value was very good for they tied down large numbers of Prussian troops and took Steyr in 1741 and Claus in 1742. Provided they were paid a bounty on results, their tasks could be extended over a wide field. On the

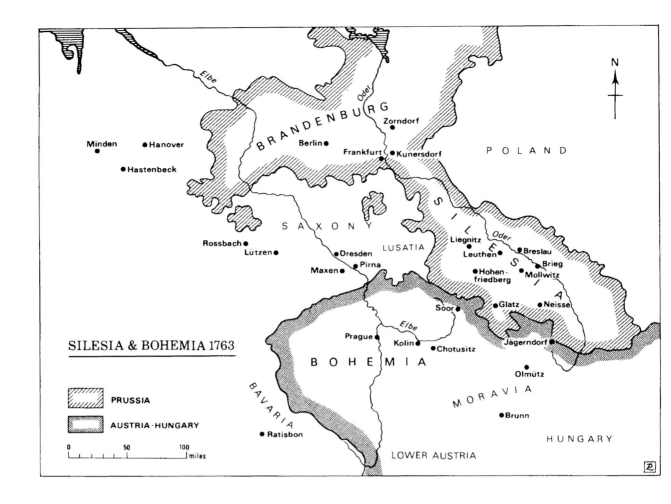

SILESIA & BOHEMIA 1763

PRUSSIA

AUSTRIA-HUNGARY

0   50   100
miles

other hand, like their leader, they were without
discipline and terrified the local population. So
much so that Field-Marshal Neipperg found
Trenck an embarrassment, particularly when
Trenck's pandours set on Neipperg's own irregulars commanded by Menzel. Trenck was arrested,
following which his pandours mutinied. Trenck
and his pandours were then removed to the command of Field-Marshal Graf Khevenhüller, who
was a pandour enthusiast, and under whom they
recommenced operations. Trenck's pandours had
much notoriety and publicity, but there were in
fact many others, all owning allegiance to their
local leaders.

Since 1535 the Christian Bosnian-Serbian
refugees from Islam, both of the Orthodox and
Roman Catholic faiths, had been allowed to
settle in the frontier areas, and there they had
been enrolled as a border guard. The newly

built fortress of Carlstadt, under the walls of
which were, so it is said, 900 Turkish skulls,
attracted Croat refugees. By 1634 these were
already providing the Austrians with a number of
cavalry squadrons and seven infantry regiments.
In 1740 the Carlstädter Generalat had a peace
strength of only several hussar and foot companies
but these had a reserve of men numbering over
20,000. By 1746 it had 800 hussars and 17,000
foot in the field. The Croat infantry totalled over
5,000 men since it consisted of four battalions each
of four companies, but the company numbered
no fewer than 240 men.

G1 General of Cavalry, winter parade uniform, c. 1760
Until 1751 the Austrian generals had freedom to
choose their own dress and, more often than not,
they wore civilian clothes. The original design
shown here was decreed by Maria Theresa in a

letter sent to general officers. Headdress, shirt, trousers and boots were uniform for all ranks of general, rank badges being shown by the number of gold-ribboned stripes (Galonnierung) on the sleeves and lower pockets of the white topcoat and waistcoat.

G2 Engineer Officer, winter field service uniform, c. 1760

Maria Theresa's corps of military engineers was small and its organization and role somewhat complicated. The main component was the Engineer Corps, which totalled only ninety-eight officers, one of whom is shown in this plate. In addition to this corps and part of the military engineer organization were the Sapper Corps and the Miner Corps, each with their own officers, maintained on separate corps lists. Except in

A well-laden carabineer carrying pickets, c. 1769

certain minor details, however, the dress of all engineer, sapper and miner officers was the same. The headdress, not shown here, was the black infantry tricorne with gold edging; the greatcoat was *dunkelhechtgrau*. The Rock half-coat was cornflower-blue, although *dunkelhechtgrau* was sometimes worn. Facings were always red.

G3 Private Soldier of Sappers, winter field service uniform, c. 1760

The corps of sappers together with the corps of pioneers carried out the main engineering tasks in the field, sometimes at the direction of the corps of engineers. Entry into the corps of sappers at this time was a haphazard business, the other ranks usually being recruited from infantry regiments detailed to provide by transfer the required number of men. In consequence they usually sent the unwanted. The cap held in the soldier's hand is the latter pattern infantry headdress with a high front and plume in red and white.

H1 Fifer of German Infantry, Summer Field Service Uniform, c. 1769

German and Hungarian infantry used the bayonet mainly for defence against cavalry. For close quarter fighting German infantry were

An artillery officer (1750–1769)

trained to use the butt of the musket as a club, wielding it by the stock, while Hungarian infantry used the short infantry pattern sabre. In 1769, when all Austro-Hungarian infantry regiments changed their titles for numbers, the grenadier companies were removed and re-formed as grenadier battalions, nineteen in all. Hungarian grenadiers and line infantry retained their traditional sabres, and the infantry sabre continued to be worn also by all German grenadiers and by German infantry bandsmen. The general-service pattern 1754 infantry musket (not shown in the plate) was easily distinguishable by its upper barrel ring and funnel shaped ramrod socket. This musician, like those in the Russian Army service, carried his fife in a metal container at his belt; his facings show that he probably came from the Neipperg Regiment, later 7 Infantry Regiment.

H2 Private Soldier of Hungarian Infantry, summer field service uniform, c. 1770

There had been numerous changes in the colouring of the uniforms of Hungarian infantry. Coats were usually white, but until 1756 waistcoats and trousers were of the regimental colour. From 1757 to about 1762 waistcoats and trousers were all blue, but from then onwards (until 1798) they reverted once more to the regimental colour. In this plate, therefore, the regimental colour of trousers and collar shows that the soldier is probably from the Palffy (19 Regiment) or the Forgäch (32 Regiment) both of which wore blue facings. The cost of the Hungarian infantry was charged to the Hungarian Exchequer except that weapons, banners, drums and tents were provided from Austrian stocks. Except that he did not wear gaiters and carried a Hungarian-pattern sabre, the Hungarian's equipment was, therefore, the same as that of the German. The Hungarian grenadier differed from infantry in that he wore a white coat with yellow facings and pale blue trousers with a yellow stripe. He had a black tall headdress surmounted by green oakleaves.

H3 Fusilier of German Infantry, summer field service uniform, c. 1769

When the grenadiers were removed from the infantry regiments, the line infantry were redesignated as fusiliers, the new name having no military significance. The infantry or fusilier company was stronger than that of grenadiers having a peace establishment of 113, and consisted of three officers and a Fähnrich, a Feldwebel, four corporals, eight Gefreite (first-class privates) and ninety-one Gemeine or fusiliers. The soldier shown in the plate wears the infantry cap, common to both German and Hungarian, and the white uniform and black gaiters worn by all German infantry.

INDEX

Figures in **bold** refer to illustrations.